The True Story of

THE YORKSHIRE
HORSEMAN

COOPER WILSON
with Chris Berry

GREAT NORTHERN

Great Northern Books
PO Box 1380, Bradford,
West Yorkshire, BD5 5FB

www.greatnorthernbooks.co.uk

ISBN: 978-1-914227-38-7

Design by David Burrill

Front cover photograph by Eleanor Wilson

CIP Data
A catalogue for this book is available from
the British Library

Welcome to my world

Contents

Introduction

Cooper Wilson is a remarkable human being. Coming from humble beginnings he is today one of the most unique and sought-after individuals in the equine world, in constant demand by horse owners who benefit from his extraordinary skills of communicative powers to understand their horses' needs.

In front of the television cameras Cooper is a quietly spoken gentleman with an affectionate smile and a glint in his eye, but away from them he is a hard-working, driven man whose sole purpose in life is to help every animal.

Cooper now spends a good deal of his time on road trips and in contact via phone readings throughout the UK and Ireland, Scandinavia, mainland Europe and the United States. He tours at the behest of organisers in each area where horses are brought to him by their owners eager to sometimes simply find out more about their horse or for Cooper to give them answers to what they perceive as problems with their dearly loved four-legged companions.

Cooper's phenomenal rise in the equine world sees him now known as the Yorkshire Horseman and revered by thousands of horse lovers all around the globe.

This book charts his incredible and compelling life story that has taken him from obscurity to his now international reputation that sees him firmly on the worldwide stage.

Chris Berry.

CHAPTER 1

The Gift

This all started with a stag. The stag has been with me throughout my life. I didn't save the stag, but it was a very early education to me about life and death and the spiritual world.

I was healing animals as a child. I didn't know that's what I was doing at the time, but I have always known that I have this gift of helping horses and during the last fifteen years this ability has led to me becoming known in many more countries and has brought about some amazing opportunities I could only have dreamed about.

Truthfully, my ability to give readings, and all of what others might call the heebie-jeebie stuff, is as much of a mystery to me why I have it, but I'm also no one-trick pony. It's not all about the readings and never has been.

I love working with horses and have worked with them for over 50 years. I've broken horses in. I've brought them back to a sense of usefulness. I've put them back in a good place. I've had times when I've had over 500 horses in my care and I have helped thousands of horses from all over the world.

That's where I am a real horseman in the truest sense of the word and that's why I have confidence in my abilities as a horseman as well as whatever other words and titles are given to me.

People call me the animal communicator and I used to shiver

when I first heard that because it over-simplifies everything. I'm not some kind of weird Doctor Doolittle.

It is impossible for a horse to actually talk, no matter how many Disney and Pixar movies you've seen and it's also impossible for me to talk back to a horse and for it to understand my words.

What my job is about is tuning in to each and every horse. There's definitely a spiritual connection and I repeat to each owner what I have seen from the horse, a lot of which comes in the form of symbols that I have to then read and make some sense of, but none of it would come at all if there wasn't a spirit world.

I never go with a script. I never go with a plan, nothing is premeditated. Doing what I do is all about being honest.

There's a saying that we live in heaven and hell on earth and that we can only make it heaven if we want to. And if the devil is ignoring you, you must be doing something wrong because he's happy with you. But if you're doing something good, he should be haunting you, so you've got to keep him out all the time. I'm just trying to make life a little more like heaven for each horse.

How the hell it all actually works I have no idea, but it definitely does as thousands will testify and keep on testifying. I most certainly believe in what I do. I believe in spirit guides and reincarnation, but I won't preach it as you can't ram any of it down folks' throats, particularly the sceptics, of whom I'd probably be one if the boot was on the other foot. I have it, that's all I know.

I just go out to do the best I can and my intention when I go out to do a reading or make a phone call is this: Is the horse happy with itself? Is it comfortable? Pain free? Is it happy in its work? And is there anything that the owner or rider can do to better it?

I never get to know any of this beforehand. I just have to have faith and trust in the spirit guides that walk with us. You can call them guardian angels if you want, but I trust them and that means I always have to say what I see.

That's something I sometimes wouldn't have done years ago for fear of what the reaction might have been from the owner, but I learned that you must always say it like it is.

I always explain this is not about reading a book or watching a film. I work with colours, symbols and sometimes words but they don't come from the horse, they come from the spirit guide. It's like a very low whisper and it's like a thought as well because where this information comes from is very close to thought.

The important thing for me is to never go in thinking I'm the man or go in with an attitude, because it really isn't all about me. It's about having faith in what you do and trusting in what you get.

You've got to respect it. If you don't, and you try to make it up yourself you will make a proper fool of yourself.

That's why I tread carefully. I take my time because you could just sweep some words out to the owner, but the information could be coming from three or four different animals and that way none of it makes sense.

I used to say that I was as rough as a yard brush and as subtle as a sledgehammer. There's still a little bit of truth in that, but I do take my time to get right what I'm being given.

My readings often don't involve seeing the horses at all, not in the first instance. It can be like an out-of-body experience where I might be standing under a tree out of the yard and yet still be working with a horse that's in the yard or in its trailer or in its stable or barn.

I will ask the owner whether my reading is on the right track, that the information I'm giving is understandable, and as long as the individual says yes I know I'm still making headway and making sense.

Sometimes it can be truly amazing because an owner can tell me it's not right, but when I keep going and say it again in a different format the owner then says it is right. It's just the way it comes to me and how that is communicated between horse, myself and the owner. It never ceases to amaze me.

What I believe people like in me is that when the horse comes out after I've given my reading I go and see it and if I've said I think it needs wedge heels on, I may correct myself because I might then see that in that horse's instance I wouldn't put a wedged heel on, as I can then see it would make the job worse. I would then give an experienced opinion on what would be right. But the important thing is that the reading is on the right track.

What I have found is that sometimes I can misunderstand the message, but that message has still put me in the correct place to sort out a problem.

I may have got the message back to front. Maybe I have mentioned an inside wall of a hoof and when I see the horse I can then tell immediately it is a problem with the outside wall. It all means I've still received the message even if I've maybe slightly misinterpreted it.

What I've also found is that you should never be too proud to say you got it wrong, because at the end of the day it's all about the welfare of the animal and helping to improve his or her ability.

My intentions are always honourable to the owner and the horse, with the horse's welfare the first priority. If I get somebody who's a bit 'mmm-err-mmm' I will always believe what I'm getting from the horse first.

The way I look at it you never fail, you just don't succeed sometimes. There's really no such thing as failure and my own personal opinion is that so long as I'm not big-headed about things, I will always succeed. That's the quiet confidence I have in my own ability to be able to do anything I want to.

When I get things wrong, I always accept that. There's also never any shame in it because my heart is in the job and my intention is to do the very best. If I get it wrong in one out of every 40 horses, where's the shame in that? That means I'm 97.5 per cent right.

Reiki helps, following the reading. My job is like a little triangle, with me, the spirit guides and the reiki. My horsemanship experience and the other two all complement one another. Reiki is a calming energy. It allows a horse to relax in his or her mind and once that is the case it is also relaxed in its body.

I have people say, "How did you do that?" when I get the horse to do what the owner often hasn't been able to, and I say, "It's all in the hands." I never fully explain it, but that's how it is.

There are some horse people who will say that horses only live in the moment, and they do, but it all depends on what you do with them and how you are with them.

I tune into horses through reiki and people often see it as intuition, but it's also that clairvoyant side for me with the reiki that helps to understand the horse's feelings and thoughts.

When a horse I have seen comes here for rehabilitation I don't bother with the heebie-jeebie stuff. I just get straight down to the horsemanship, because there are only certain places you need to use that other stuff. It's about knowing when you need it and when you don't. Back home I'm Cooper Wilson, the horseman, nothing more, just working with the horses.

It's a fulfilling job. I make them better or, at the very least, make their lives happier and healthier when sometimes all hope from their owner has gone and that is reflected in their manner.

What I am getting is the pleasure and satisfaction from being with horses. Like anything that is your passion and your true vocation it isn't about money, it is about job satisfaction. I've never had a lot of it (money) but what I have is the satisfaction and that's what brings true happiness. The world could be falling to pieces, like it seems to be right now, but I'd still have that.

Some horses have ability and some haven't. Some horses are in the wrong job, just like people, and it causes stress.

These days my phone never stops ringing and I am now almost constantly on tour with road trips, but if I can help make a difference over the phone I don't see why it shouldn't be done. When I'm not on tour I'm on with phone readings. On a phone call it's all spirit guide stuff and you get a vision in your mind's eye.

The people who come to my readings when I'm on my road trips today are now largely in my camp, but years ago when I first started they weren't.

At that time there were many who were more than sceptical. Some thought I was some kind of fairground attraction equivalent to a fortune teller, others were deeply unkind and discourteous.

I've had experiences where people have got me to their place to try and make me look a fool. Heaven knows why, but I guess hell does, and within seconds I've been thinking I know what you're about. In years gone by I would have defended myself, but today I just walk away from it. It really is their problem, not mine.

In those days I would feel that I had to go even deeper to prove my worth. I would ask my spirit guides, but what I received back was reassuring and with simple instructions that have stood me in good stead throughout.

I was told very simply to 'see no evil, hear no evil' and informed not to react to any provocation or inflammatory remarks other than to say to whoever was instigating the negativity, that there is something in what I do. I will always stand my ground.

I'm always very nice to people. I respect them, whoever they are. Mum always said that you should always tip your cap to everybody, because you don't know who they are. I agree with the first part, but the second part really isn't important. I've found that you should be just as civil as you can be to everybody regardless of how much money they have or rank they hold in society.

One thing I do know is that this old rose will always get back up and bloom. I will always stand up and be counted.

I've not lived a boring life.

If you had a ping pong ball and threw it against a wall and it bounced that's how my life has been. I've been up, I've been down – but right now I am in the right place.

And before we move on with my story, I must stress that I am not a vet and that I must always advise that if your horse has problems you should always contact your vet.

Right, let's get back to that stag.

CHAPTER 2

The Stag

I am the third-born child, or fourth dependent on how you look at it, of Tom and Mary Wilson.

Dad was born in Wigton in Cumbria and left home when he was 13 to work on a farm. He was from a big family of farm labourers who were from Irish blood.

Dad met my mum, then Mary Garcia, in Longtown, while he worked as a groom with point-to-point horses and hunters.

My grandfather was Clem Garcia. Clem's father, my great grandfather, had originally come from Argentina to Mexico and then to Texas where he'd met and married an indigenous North American lady.

Clem and Mary had ten children, including my mum.

I once saw a picture of my grandma and she was an olive colour. My mother was the same. We used to call her Spanish because of it.

When you look back in my ancestry, my great grandfather on my mother's side was from South America; my grandma was some form of indigenous North American and very spiritual and there's Irish blood on my father's side. So, if anyone wanted to look into what makes me what I am, perhaps those bloodlines might make some sense.

Firstborn of my siblings was my eldest brother Rodney, who sadly passed away in 2018. Next up were twins Edna and Jack.

Jack was still-born, hence the third- or fourth-born bit. My mother could never talk about him, but I sometimes feel Jack working with me, and my grandfather Clem. They are both strong spiritual presences in my world. After I was born came my other two sisters Charlotte and Aileen.

I was born on 11 February 1961 on the cusp of South Yorkshire and North Nottinghamshire. At the time my father was a hunt servant to the Grove & Rufford Hunt at Barnby Moor near Retford where he was employed by the master of the hounds. He had been with the Cumberland Farmers Hunt previously.

A hunt servant was a bit like a butler to a big house. The hunt servant would look after the hounds and he would 'whip in' to a huntsman. My father said the hunting game was an entertainment for the rich and our job was to supply the entertainment.

There's a saying in the hunt world that the first year you settle in, the second year you have a good year and often the third too, but the fourth becomes a bad one because they fall out with you. We moved around the country quite a bit.

It was when I was three or maybe four years old, when Dad was with the Hampshire Hunt, that I had my first spiritual experience. We lived in a thatched cottage.

I remember it like it was yesterday and it has stayed with me throughout my life, not as some kind of traumatic and haunting thing but as something that has, when I look back on it now, shaped the rest of my life.

I walked out of our garden and across the yard. I was barefoot and had no shirt on. That's some memory, I know. I can't tell you what time of year it was, but it wasn't cold; either that or I was a tough nut, like we are from up here in Yorkshire.

I was standing at the corner of this building and I saw a stag being shot. It had been involved in a traffic accident. I can't tell you what had happened because I hadn't been there to witness that, but it must have run out into the country lane right in front of an oncoming vehicle or something like that, because it had been shot to put it out of its misery.

But that's when I saw something more.

As I was standing there, I haven't just seen the stag, lifeless, I've also seen it stood, proud and alive, its spiritual energy.

This was the start of my spiritual mind. I understood straight away about the stag being killed, about it dying. I'm not stupid. Not even at three or four years old. But because I'd also seen its spiritual energy it empowered me rather than scared me.

I didn't know it at the time, but I was already working out in my own mind about life and death, and what happens after we die. Life doesn't end with our physical death; it is just part of the journey we're going through.

That's what I'd worked out by the time I was five years old.

I have never forgotten the stag and as I grew older I would often see other spirits, like the spirit of a woman or a man walking through a door into a room. It happened regularly and I was never scared of it and sometimes these people, these spirits, would talk to me.

When I was younger, I'd sometimes say something to whoever was there at the time, like "What's up with her?" thinking that I was seeing something others could see. I'd get something back like, "There's nobody there, what are you on about?"

But the purpose of telling you all of this is not to get too whacky, but that I would start knowing things about animals, like when a horse was going to go lame.

CHAPTER 3

Horses & Me

I will always have horses in my world. They have been the one constant in my life. They don't employ a class system, they respond positively to kindness, they don't try to trick you, they don't play any of the silly games that sometimes happens in the world of human beings.

It is horses that have shown me how to love, how to live and how to understand emotions. If I ever need to find comfort, to find my way back from a dark place, it is always through horses.

Horses helped when I was younger with all of the moves we had from one hunt to another. We moved from the Hampshire Hunt to the Berwickshire and then to the Atherstone in Warwickshire, all within just a few years. When that happens it is hard to make friends, as no sooner are you settled in somewhere than you are off again.

We had a number of upheavals and the move from school to school was at times distressing. I had three schools in a short time. You learn how to make friends, but then in making friends you sometimes learn that some people aren't as honest as they first appear.

My schooltime at Atherstone was one of my better ones. I'd settled into that school and I'd made some good friends. There was Barbara Hyatt, George Hyatt and Timothy Bird, Stephen Sawser and Helen Scattergood, the headmistress's daughter.

George was my best friend.

It was the 1960s, or maybe just into 1970, and fallen stock would be brought in to where we lived. It could be anything. Cows and horses for instance. They weren't exactly fallen in the sense that they were dead, they were stock that their owners just wanted rid of. Their eventual slaughter would be to provide the hounds with fresh flesh, but in the meantime they would graze nearby.

I used to go with these horses in the field, those whose time was said to be nearly up. They'd often been classed as dangerous or crippled.

I would be a young boy of eight, nine or ten years old. The horses' owners may have sent them because they either had a problem or had proven too difficult to handle and I used to mess around with them. I used to plait string and make a bridle and ride them bareback.

There was this one horse that had come in because he'd allegedly been a dangerous horse, but I'd been playing in the field with him and had got to know him. I had faith in this horse, I rode him. I understood him. The horse got to trust me, and I trusted the horse.

These were times when I was learning that there's far more to a horse than four legs and a head, which is what most people see.

This horse would do anything for me. I'd jump poles with him, trot circles, anything he wanted and all with just an old bit of billy band or string. There were knots everywhere, but he'd do everything, and he'd let me because we had that trust.

One Christmas Day I decided to ride him down to the village to say Happy Christmas to Helen. Timothy Bird lived next door to her too. I put a string bridle on to this horse and he had an old bit in his mouth. The horse was 16 hands and I was only a dot of a thing. I'm not much different now come to think of it.

Next thing I know, my dad's coming down the road and he says, "What the bloody hell do you think you're doing on that? You'll get yourself killed!"

"Oh," I said, quite innocently and honestly. "He came down that hill like a good 'un." I wasn't trying to go against my dad. It was just a natural response as myself and the horse were good together.

He said, "It came in to be put down because it's dangerous."

I said, "He's not." But again, I didn't say it as though I was going against his word. I was merely stating fact as I saw it. Even back then they made mistakes with horses, about whether they were wrong 'uns or not.

I said, "I'll ride him back." But my dad, who was also being reasonable, said, "I dare not let you."

While we were at Atherstone I also had my first altercation with a vet. Now, I will say this here and now, loud and clear, I respect vets. I'm not one myself. I'm self-taught on all I know about animals.

I know many vets, many of whom are good friends and they truly know their stuff, they are knowledgeable people who care about animals, but there is also a place for those from the spiritual world, particularly those who have first-hand experience with animals every day, like me.

I must have been around nine or ten years old when a vet visited and said this particular horse was lame.

I said, "No it's not, it's wrong there," and I put my finger on its tendon. I said, "It's there, it's got a hole in it."

At the time I didn't know the name to be able to say that it was the tendon. I said to the vet that it should just be chucked in the field and that it would come right in time. That was my spiritual side.

You can imagine what the vet thought about being told how

to do his job from a young kid, but I'd only given an honest account. I wasn't after his job or wanting to win any kind of acclaim – and I certainly didn't get it!

This vet said, "Poppycock!" All very English, but to give him his due when he investigated, there was a hole there in the tendon. The vet just said he reckoned I'd made a lucky guess.

Then we had this little old black mare come in that was crippled with arthritis. She and I got on really well. I got to understand her emotions. This is where I was learning that horses can really love back, and they can respond positively.

I didn't know exactly what I was doing, but I knew that what I was doing was making a difference and that I was making her more comfortable.

When I came back home from school one day I went straight to see this horse in the field with a few others. I'd grown fond of the old girl, but she wasn't there. She had gone. They'd put her to sleep for flesh for the hounds – which was why she had been there after all.

I was a bit upset about it, but I was a hunt servant's son and I understood what it was about. I found comfort in the thought that at least her last weeks had been happy.

It took me back to the stag. When I'd seen it after it had been shot its spirit had looked well and happy. I felt that the old mare would now feel the same and had moved on to another world.

I made connections with all of these horses, that were all eventually put down, but because of the stag and the horses I had experiences that gave me another world to be in and that kept me sane, particularly when my school life wasn't so good.

Horses and me. That's the way everything was going to be.

CHAPTER 4

Victorian

My father was very Victorian in his ways and we lived a very Victorian hard life. It was that kind of way in those days when the class system in this country, particularly in the countryside, saw my dad and our family as the lowest of the low.

I was told, by my dad, when I got to about ten years old that I should hear all, see all, but say nowt. You had to keep your mouth shut and you were made to feel that your opinion was not valid. I was told to be seen but not heard. That was the life we led.

It was a class thing. We were hunt servants. Dad wasn't on a big wage. Others looked down on you, so you didn't get involved, you had to stand back. And as I got a little older I remember being called useless and being looked down on by what they used to call the gentry.

These people would never praise you, even when you had done well, but I knew that what I was doing was right and I didn't want thanking for it. That's something that I've noticed in the human world. Everyone wants thanking for everything they do right.

It is an awful thing for anyone to be made to feel that they are useless and to be ridiculed just because you don't have the same opportunities as some.

I feel for people today who are caught up in poverty and

sometimes a world where they struggle to find a way out and true happiness.

It was the same for me at school, especially after I'd left the infants and junior school I'd been at first in Atherstone. I'd had a lot of friends when I was at junior school, but in the one year I had at Market Bosworth when I was 11 years old I only had two friends – Michelle Lambert and Barry Brotherhood.

Where it all went horribly wrong and where I learned how cruel people can be was when we moved to Wooler in Northumberland.

I was bullied at school in Wooler, but if you know anything about me by now you will know that for a little wiry guy with jug ears and who looked a bit like I'd grown up in the gutter, or at least in a field, I was never going to be some kind of meek and mild kid. I was never going to let them run over me.

As children at home, we were all well fed, that much was never an issue. My mum made the best meals, but because we never had much money, we were all poorly clothed.

I would go to school at Wooler with black wellies on, with my trousers over the top. I had my hair done short back and sides, had big ears like elephants', and I was small. That was easy pickings for bullies, or at least they thought so.

If you've ever been picked on at school or work just remember this. Always be better than them, those that pick on you, the bullies. There is truly something wrong with them, not you. It is their lives that are missing something, not yours.

My brother Rodney went through the same as me, but his mental strength couldn't cope with it and he ended up with a mental health problem all his life. He would go with the wrong 'uns to try and fit in, but I didn't need that.

I had horses and I knew that I made a difference to their

lives, that I had a worth. I knew I had these in my life and that I didn't need anybody.

When you know that what you do can make a difference and you know that what you do is making life better for someone or something, like a horse or a cow or a ewe, it is what life is really about.

So, if you are someone young and at school at the moment and you are reading this book and you've just been bullied, think of all that you are and what you can do that truly makes a difference in this world and I truly hope that makes you smile and gives you some comfort.

Now, I'm not advocating violence and I'm not saying this next bit is the best way to behave, but if these bullies thought they were going to make my life hell they were about to find out that this little lad had far more about him than they thought.

When I was at school in Wooler there was this lad who was a real 24-carat bully. He used to stab me in the back with the point of his pencil as we queued to go back into school after dinner. I'm sure he thought it was absolutely hilarious. He'd be laughing with his mates about it, but I never gave him the satisfaction of turning round, until one day when he took it a step too far.

That day he used the point of a compass instead. That was it for me. This lad was poking me with his compass, so I turned so fast he didn't see what was coming. I grabbed him by the throat.

One thing I had learned back at home is that when you hold something, you hold it firm. And I locked on to him so hard he was shocked.

I took him out of the line, still holding him by the throat and I hit him hard. I dropped him like he had been shot and gave him the biggest beating he had ever had. I beat the living daylights out of him. I might only have been a little feller but I was strong. I was like a little bull.

And you know what? Not one of his so-called friends came to his rescue. Not one. Nobody helped him out. And I didn't get banned either, but I started distancing myself from people. It wasn't good for me, but I wasn't going to be bullied, that was for sure.

I ended up not going to school as much as I should. Who would want to, given the circumstances where you are getting constantly bullied? Again, I'm not advocating this to anyone. It was just the way it was for me.

Like a lot of young kids on farms or working with horses I was working at home in the early hours before catching the bus to school. I was working alongside my dad quite often from being about 13 years old and despite his Victorian ways, or maybe because of them, I liked being with him.

I never learned to read or write properly. That's why I got Chris (Berry) to write this book for me in the way that I speak, because I can't do it for myself.

Everything I have learned has come from either my parents, from people I've worked with, people I've watched, hands-on with horses or from the spiritual world.

When I had been at school at Wooler for about six months my teacher asked about my homework, saying that none of it made any sense. It didn't. I told him that I couldn't read or write and that I'd never been able to. It had only taken him six months to work that one out.

But, like a lot of people who can't read or write, one thing I was good at was Maths. When I had been at school in Market Bosworth I'd have the answer to a sum by the time the teacher had written it up on the board. And I also found that I could speak French and Spanish.

We moved from Wooler to Scarborough when dad took up a job with the Derwent Hunt and I moved to Scalby School. It was the same story there as at Wooler, but by then I'd really pretty much given up on school apart from showing my face every now and again.

That's when I started doing more work for the hunt, at the kennels with Dad, back at home. I was happier there.

Through the summer months before the summer holiday came around, I'd be up in a morning before I went to school and I'd get the horses ready to go out and exercise them, then I'd muck out, and then I'd go and catch the bus. Sometimes I'd deliberately miss it.

When I got back at night I would groom the horses, muck out and put everything back in place that had been used during the day.

If you're squeamish just skip the next few lines because after that I'd start skinning the animals that had been slaughtered that day, ready to provide the fresh flesh for the hounds.

This was my form of studying. This was where I had taken myself right out of what was considered to be the normal world of education.

I was still going to school, but it was all getting a bit hit and miss.

My education was right here at home. Kids at school might see bits of things in jars and call it biology, but I was learning real anatomy and was getting to know it at close quarters.

When the vet would come, I'd stand, listen and watch. That's how I learned the anatomy of a horse – the joints, the ligaments – it was all by listening to the vets.

One of my jobs was to dress a horse down so that when the

vet turned up, I would open it up and the vet would look at the internal organs. I'd learn how to dress the legs and how to do a post-mortem. How to bring the tendon down through its layers, so that you could see the internal ligament.

I was skinning and learning about anatomy all at the same time. I was skinning everything from sheep to calves, cows and horses, all for feed for the hounds.

I'd go to school two or three days a week and by the time I was 15 I was in trouble with what they used to call the Kiddie Catchers who would be sent by the school authorities to get you back into school.

They would come and my mother was a bit blunt with them. In fact, she was a bit more than blunt. Colourful language along the lines of telling them to go forth and multiply, or words that imply that. You didn't upset my mother. If Dad was hard and Victorian in his ways, Mum was even harder.

I was in trouble one day after the Kiddie Catchers had been and I was met with the full force of Mum and the frying pan! Right in my face! It nearly knocked my eyebrows off, and all Mum said was, "You'll do as you are told from now on!"

I went back to school, not out of any kind of loyalty to the school or because of my mum, but to try and convince them that I was the better person. Or maybe, thinking about it, it was because I didn't want whacking with my mum's frying pan again!

But by then I knew what I was good at already, and I knew I was doing well with the horses.

There were loads of horses that came into us at home while we were with the Derwent that I made a complete difference with, and cows as well. It all helped make me more independent and in my own little world.

I also knew that what I was doing was right and that I didn't need thanking for it. I knew I was good with animals.

Mind you, it was also a good job that I didn't need thanking because Dad never gave me any praise.

But I mean what I say, when I say that I didn't need the praise. In a way I was just like my dad. We both got on with our work and just wanted to do a good job. We would both know when we had done so and when you have that confidence you don't need others to give it to you.

Dad was largely ignorant to the good work I was doing, until he sometimes took credit for it, but that's just the sort of person my dad was. Not bad, just very Victorian.

I got on with him like a house on fire. I wasn't bothered about the credit. I've always thought that when you know you've done a good job nobody can take it away from you.

Dad's Victorianism also led to me always having to call him 'sir', not Dad, when we were out together. At home I could be as daft as I liked. But outside the house it was always 'sir'.

CHAPTER 5

Early Successes

Even in my teens I was starting to raise eyebrows among the horse community when they saw what I was doing. It wasn't like I was getting particularly well known or that I was getting any praise, it was just that people would see horses and cows they'd sent to us getting better.

This was way before any of the heebie-jeebie stuff that some people think I'm all about today. It was way before I even knew what reiki was, and it just showed that what I had came naturally, as well as spiritually.

Now some of you younger people, who I hope are reading this book and are hopefully reassured of your own talents, will perhaps be experiencing similar things in your lives.

Maybe you are on a farm or with a family in the countryside where you work well with horses. Maybe you will see some similarities. I hope this book helps you because we know we are different, don't we? We really do have something very special in our lives.

Here are some of my early successes with horses as a teenager:

A farmer once sent us a pony in called Diamond. It was a little scruffy thing, only 14.2 hands and it had been regarded as dangerous, so it had been sent to be put to sleep. Diamond was basically on Death Row. He was due to go when fresh flesh was needed for the hounds.

I soon found out that whoever had sent it, had been right. You couldn't ride one side of it at all. It was properly gone in the head, but I got to know it. I helped it and by the time I'd finished I could not only ride it, I could also hunt it. And boy could this thing operate!

It started to go so well that my dad began hunting with the hounds off it and jumping five-bar gates too.

And blow me, the people who had sent it in, saw what I'd done and said they'd have it back! The feller who'd sent it, said to me, "You've got that pony going well, do you think my daughter will be able to ride it like you?"

Dad said he should take it and find out.

They took it and what a pony it was! It went on to be brilliant. For me it was great. I'd done the work, what I had considered to be the right communication with the horse, I'd shown it trust and kindness. And I'd saved Diamond from Death Row!

On what is a funnier side looking back now, I have a picture of me riding Diamond with the hunt and the clothes I'm wearing, deary me, it's like what shop did he get them at?

The hunting jacket I wore didn't fit and wasn't even a real hunting jacket. It was a suit jacket. And it wasn't mine. I never had the money to buy the correct clothing, so I looked a right scruff.

And just in case you're also starting to think that I'm trying to say everything I do has always been right with horses, here's something I learned along the way with Diamond – and it could have been a far different story for him if the owner had seen me with him that day.

I put a saddle on him for the first time at the Derwent and boy did I struggle to ride him at first. The saddle kept slipping off. We were going up this dale and the saddle went up its neck.

I was at the front of the hunt and because I'd got frustrated with the saddle, he'd got frustrated.

The horse got panicky and I gave him a slap.

Ooh, that was a big mistake. All I did was slap him, but he reacted the way anyone might, if they are hit. He was shocked and it unsettled him even more. If I'd wanted to get the old Diamond back, which clearly I didn't want to do, this was one sure way of doing it.

That's when I learned never ever to hit a horse again and that anger doesn't cure anything.

I was 13. I'm not making excuses by using my age. I knew instantly I had a job on to get him back calmed down. All my good work was in danger of going down the pan.

I jumped off and threw the saddle in the hedge back. He was hard to settle for a while afterwards.

This was a very important moment. I hadn't intended it to be that way, of course, but I dealt with the situation.

It was proof to me that arguing and fighting, setting things off wrongly and holding grudges doesn't work. Once again, if you're young and reading this I hope it helps. From my own personal experience nothing good comes from it. It's far better to be positive and be happy.

Diamond and I worked well again after that. I never went back for the saddle though, and we carried on bareback for the remainder of that day.

We had another horse – also being sent to Death Row. It was a big Anglo Arab stallion. A giant among horses. I'm not kidding. His owners hadn't been able to do anything with him, but I had him doing everything.

I could ride him bareback with a bit of string around his neck, take him out from the paddock, through the fields. He'd jump clear over this stone wall from the road. He'd canter away and I could tell he loved it. It's all about connecting with the animal.

The person who'd had him hadn't adjusted to his needs. He needed bigger things to jump over. He loved the challenge. He'd been getting frustrated at not being able to have the opportunity. I could tell. Maybe the owner had been scared about jumping. Me and horses again.

But, like I say, it's not just horses I connect with.

I remember once a cow came into the kennels to be put to sleep. It had foot rot. I'd be about 13–14 years old.

The old girl couldn't put her foot down. She was another on Death Row just waiting for her number to be up, but fortunately fresh flesh wasn't needed just at that time.

I said I would milk it to keep it from getting mastitis. Dad wasn't a cruel man. He said I should look after the cow until they were ready for it. He was very mindful of the care of animals. That's where I get it from.

I had no real idea exactly what I was going to do with this cow, but I set about cleaning its foot with saltwater. I was working on the theory of seawater being good for racehorses. We were near the coast, so I went to Scarborough with a five-gallon drum to collect saltwater.

I used to then soak the foot in seawater, and blow me again, this cow came healthy, put weight on and we were milking her and having some of it for breakfast. It was really good stuff and for a time she became our house cow, like many farmers used to have.

The farmer at Broxby who had sent it in, came riding by the kennels one day and saw the cow in the field. On his way back he called in and said, "When are you going to put that cow down?"

My dad said that the cow's foot was back right and that we were milking it to provide milk for the hounds' pups.

The farmer said: "Right. I'll pick it back up next Tuesday and take it to Malton (livestock market) to the auctions."

I never got thanked for it, my dad got all the praise and Chris, the farmer, got a lot of money for it! At least the cow was saved. Another one escaping the clutches of Death Row!

But I got the most of everything out of it because I got the experience. All this time I was building up this experience with animals and it was creating greater confidence in myself.

I was learning all the time and I knew in myself that I was making a difference. These horses and cows. I was showing they could have a quality of life. I didn't use that phrase at that time. Back then I just said that they could do something.

It was all about me and them. The horses and the cows. Nobody hassled me over it either, because nobody knew what I was doing. I was just working with animals. Me and horses or me and cows. I wasn't reading things up in books about how you should or shouldn't do things, because I couldn't read anyway. But most importantly of all I was allowing the animal to express itself.

I was 12 years old when I broke in my first pony and boy did it turn into a great success for me, both for my personal pride and, as it turned out, my confidence, although my setting of a price obviously needed a lot of work.

I'd bought him for 26 guineas at Seamer Horse Fair. I used to make a few quid delivering what I shovelled back home on to people's gardens, and I'd save the money I earned to buy a pony.

At the time of buying him I had no idea that my work would turn out so successful that it would even make me money. I hadn't looked at it that way at all. I just liked working with horses.

After breaking him, I took him out hunting and the following day a man called Charles Chafer came down to see me and said, "I do like that pony. I think you've done a wonderful job with him and I was wondering whether you would like to sell him because I'd like my granddaughter to have him, he showed such good temperament when I saw him yesterday."

I said, "Yes, I'd sell him," and Mr Chafer asked how much I would like for him.

I said, really seriously, "Well I gave £25 for him …"

That's how much of a businessman I was at 12 years old.

Thankfully, Mr Chafer was an honourable man and was not about to take liberties with a young lad who was clearly a bit wet behind his very large ears!

Mr Chafer was very gracious and said, "Well, for the work you've put into him I think you need a little bit more than that. I'm going to write a cheque out in your name and let's see if you're happy with it."

It was for £360!

"Would that be enough?" he said.

Too right it would! Mr Chafer handed it to me and I understand his granddaughter had Timmy, as he became known, for the rest of his life.

And while money is certainly not everything, nor was it what drove me to work more with horses, Timmy was by no means the only financial success during my years as a teenager.

I was about 14–15 years old when a pony, that I gave the name Sparky, came into the kennels at Snainton to be destroyed, another one for Death Row. His number almost definitely up.

Sparky was classed as a runaway. He was regarded as dangerous. Oh my, did I work with Sparky.

Once again, it was all about getting to know the horse's

needs. My father always said you had to respect the animal you were working with and meet its needs, regardless of its outcome. Those words have stayed with me right through my life.

I got Sparky right. I hunted him and he turned out to be an amazing jumper, another horse that had been frustrated in not being able to do what he had wanted to previously or had not been handled the way in which it suited his personality.

All horses have their own personality, their own talents. They differ from horse to horse. That's what many people don't truly understand. Just like us, horses are not the same.

Sparky was a wonderful horse, not a runaway at all. I remember jumping a stone wall on him that must have been 4ft that dropped into where, within a handful of strides, he jumped a 3ft hedge out again. It is really all about knowing how to deal with a horse's mental ability.

Once you've mastered that, the horse's physical ability comes clear, as it did that day. This was one very talented horse that was now enjoying life.

I hunted him a whole season and we sold him at the end of hunting season to a family in Leeds. My father got £1,000 for him!

Me and horses. Sparky, Timmy, Diamond and many more. I saved quite a few from where they had been destined to go – I learned how to listen to horses, how to rehabilitate horses.

My childhood and teenage years weren't your average child's experiences of life. They were, in my humble opinion, wonderful years in learning just how much I had in my life that others might never have.

CHAPTER 6

The Milk Horses:
My Point-to-Point Career

I had dreams of being a National Hunt racehorse jockey, but that's where it started and ended.

It wouldn't have mattered how many horses I had worked with or how many I had given a new lease of life back home. That counted for nothing.

I tried. It's not as though I didn't give it a go, but we had no horses of our own. We were too poor to afford to keep any ourselves and we were certainly not able to afford anything that might run well. Those that were in the top bracket already had their riders, either because of family connections, money or past record. I had none of that.

All of my pointing happened in the mid-70s and I was given all the milk horses, all the no-hopers. I never even got round once, as most of them never got to the open ditch.

Who knows? Maybe looking back I should have stuck around a little longer and if I had, maybe I'd have been given a better ride.

I rode at Charm Park and at Sinnington, maybe a handful of rides altogether and all in just one season.

I considered myself a good rider, a good prospect as a jockey, but you can only do so much with a horse that hasn't got it in it. The posher kids and the established jockeys of the day had all the rides sewn up between them.

Some horses have ability and some haven't, as I keep making the point; and for some it is just not in their DNA, in the same way we are all made differently, so they are too.

You might ask why some of these horses were really racing or not, but that happens everywhere. Some of the horses I rode just didn't want to be there, but their owners wanted them to be and it was they who called the shots, totally oblivious to the fact it wasn't meant to be.

In the end I didn't queue up for any more rides. I just felt it wasn't worth the risk, getting injured on something that didn't stand a chance anyway. Where's the fun in that?

I could have raced on the flat, but I didn't want to because it didn't do anything for me.

The challenge of riding horses is to be a team, to achieve, and with jump racing you've really got to work with your horse, understand your horse, and you get to see it for what it is. I'm sure that's also true for riding horses on the flat that go like the wind, it's just my preference and what I have been used to.

To me there's always been more of an art to being a jump jockey, as there is eventing or show jumping, and the more you understand your horse and adjust to it the more successful you will be.

But was it really an early end to my racing career?

CHAPTER 7

Stable Lad:
The John Travolta Period

I was always very loyal to my father. I was his right-hand man from being 13 to 21 years of age. I worked as a kennelman and by the time I was 21 I was on the princely sum of £22 per week.

We were working for the York & Ainsty North for this gentleman (I use the title for him very loosely) who was the only person in the world I will never forgive because he was absolutely horrible to my father.

He was horrible to me too, but it was the way in which he made my father's life a living hell that is why I could never forgive him. It didn't matter massively to me. I was always going to move away from the living that my father had chosen, but I stayed as long as I could to support him.

By now I had reached an age when I had that inner confidence that comes from knowing that I could do something that somebody else couldn't. I was getting wise to my ability and to that special bond I had with horses and other animals and although I was still too young to realise just where it would lead to, I knew I had to get away.

Just in case you're wondering whether there has ever been much more in my life than horses, well not really, although *Saturday Night Fever* and *Grease* had a lot to answer for, for a short while.

While we were still at Snainton, before we had moved over to the York & Ainsty North, and when I was about 18, I would go out into Scarborough on Saturday nights. We'd go on the seafront and on to a nightclub.

I'd never have thought about going, but how it had come about was that this woman had wanted a horse for her son and he and I had become good pals. Rob (Staveley), known as 'Blink' was a bit of a night owl, loved going out and stopping out late and so I tagged along with him. I met his friends and got to know them. They were alright and I liked the music at that time.

They knew I was the country lad who wasn't really used to this kind of world, so when I was in the nightclub they would look after me. It was good to have people around me like that. I'd not really had that at school since I'd been little.

Fortunately, by now, I wasn't dressed like I would have been at home. I didn't go in wellies, but I had to borrow my brother's shoes because I didn't have any normal ones and I certainly didn't have the money to buy any latest fashion.

But I was no John Travolta either in what I wore, how I looked or how I danced. Oh dear me, no. I never had girls wanting me to dance with them. I didn't have girlfriends, but I wasn't bothered either.

I've always enjoyed music though. At that time, it was all about John Travolta and disco stuff. When I was at home, I remember really liking songs that were already old even then, like 'Crying in the Rain' by the Everly Brothers, a bit of Elvis Presley and Jim Reeves.

If you watch some of the videos of horses on my Facebook page you'll quite often hear some great country music songs as background music, but I also like songs like 'Meet You Halfway' by the Black Eyed Peas.

When I finally finished at the kennels, which was the same time my father finished too, I decided to pursue my career with horses the way in which many have done before me and continue to do to this day. I became a stable lad.

I worked for a number of racehorse trainers over about a six-year period and some of them reminded me too much of the same aristocratic Victorian carry-on I'd already experienced with my father.

I worked for Jimmy Fitzgerald and Pat Rohan. They were both alright. Jimmy said he thought I was a good horseman, that was praise indeed as I respected him, but David Chapman was simply the best for me and who we will come to soon. I was with another trainer for only a week, but the one that I really did not hit it off with was a trainer we will call Fortescue Upham here. It suits him.

One or two of these trainers had offended me, because they weren't appreciating what I could do for them with their horses. At that time being young and maybe a bit full of myself too, I was starting to reckon I at least deserved a little respect.

What some had seen was that I was good with a bad horse, and so I was always given the one that needed a lot of work. I didn't mind that.

I was the stable lad who became the suicide jockey, because all the other stable lads and lasses gave the bad horses a massive swerve.

I didn't need thanking for what I was doing, I just needed respect and I definitely didn't have it from Fortescue Upham.

It all came to a head one day when I was riding this horse from his stables. It wasn't one of the horses I would normally ride. It wasn't a suicide ride. What I'd seen when it had been going up the gallops with this other lad was that it wasn't doing the tap.

I said, "You're not doing this horse any favours you know. It will never make a racehorse this way."

I'd seen that this horse was wrong in its back, that's why it had been going up sideways.

For once I got a ride on this thing and for once I'd got a decent horse under me and we went up the gallops settled and in a straight line because of the way I held it. The horse then started to move really well, the best it had done for the yard, it was like a proper racehorse for the first time. I had to admit I was dead chuffed with myself.

So, I'm walking the horse back into the yard and this thing had never come back to the yard dry and relaxed.

This time it came back with me bone dry. I had my feet out of the irons. The world was good. I knew I'd done the right thing.

I don't know that I was smiling outwardly but I was definitely smiling on the inside. Maybe I was even ready for some kind of acknowledgement. I certainly didn't get it from Fortescue Upham.

He always met everything coming into the yard at the gates.

I was just about to say something to him like, "This went well," when he said, "If I see you riding that horse like that again I'll knock you off it."

Technically that's not word for word what he said because there will hopefully be children reading this book and his vile language is best left where he deserves to be, in the gutter, but this man had and still has money.

I was young, no doubt a little full of myself at what I had just achieved, well aware of my ability with horses and not about to take his disgraceful language towards me.

I threw the reins over the horse's head and said, "If you can ride the thing any better ride it yourself." And I jumped off, got in my car and drove off. That was the last time I ever rode for him and I have never wanted to go back to him since for anything. Vile men reap what they sow.

I rang him later and asked about my wages. He said, smug and pompous as you like, "If you're brave enough to come back for them." There was never any doubt of that. The initial letters of his name here sum up my feeling towards him. Vile man.

I had a few jobs away from being a stable lad before I got a job with David Chapman at Stillington.

Stable lad is what I'd wanted to be.

What I knew, and what I've always known, is that I just wanted to be with horses more than people.

David seemed like a nice chap when I first met him and working for him proved the best move I ever made. Any man or woman in their right mind would have been extremely grateful of the fantastic job you would have with David. I certainly was. I was given more respect, more help, more understanding from David than I had experienced anywhere else in my life.

I used to ride a lot of horses for him, and he knew I could ride the dodgy ones too, but he didn't give them to me because of me being this so-called suicide jockey. He knew I could do a job, and he was also very good with dodgy horses himself. It was David who set a very good example to me as a horseman.

He would talk with me. I'd never actually had that before. I'd had to learn everything myself up until then. My father had never shown that much interest in talking about horses in any depth. David would talk with me so much.

I would sometimes ask him what he was looking for, because I was questioning my own ability, and then he'd tell me. More often than not I'd then say, "I was looking for the same thing." We were kindred spirits.

The best way I can describe it is when he and I were seeing a horse working up and down the gallops I'd ask what he was looking for? It was reassuring for me that I was looking for the same thing. He was a man to watch, the way he worked and the way he assessed. We got on. And he also had me on the best wages I'd ever had, at £124 per week.

Most importantly though, it was David who gave me my chance and I will be forever grateful. David could see what I could do. He's no longer with us, but he's still with me in the spiritual world. And he's still talking to me about horses.

Unfortunately, there were one or two lads and lasses in the yard who saw me as his blue-eyed boy and sadly they got a bit jealous which led to me having to leave David's yard through what happened.

Heaven preserve me from people and their ways. Give me horses any day!

CHAPTER 8

Broken Neck:
And Other Broken Bones

I had a terrible accident at David Chapman's yard. Some of the staff had got a little bit jealous of my relationship that they had seen blossom with David and were trying to make things difficult for me.

It was stuff I could deal with. They would frighten a horse by coming behind it while I was holding it or when I was either getting in the saddle or already up top. It didn't faze me.

The incident that broke me was all down to a girl, who I know just wanted me out of the way.

This girl was in the yard breaking horses in and she said that I needed to get on these horses to do them some good, but the thing was that I knew they weren't ready.

I told her that she needed to do more work with them. She didn't like that. She thought she knew best, but I could see the way they were, and to my mind this girl was cutting corners. I could see she was trying me out, reckoning that if I was supposedly that good with tricky horses I should be able to handle them.

She went to David and said that I was refusing to ride them. She was just trying to make life difficult for me. Little did she know how difficult my life was going to be for me just a short while later, but I guess she couldn't care less.

I said to David, "They're not ready, sir," (I always called him 'sir') "taking them now will spoil the work already being done with the horses." And I turned to the one that she was really now pushing me to ride.

"You can't push that horse," I said. "It will be a good horse given the proper time, but this one is not ready yet."

I think David must have felt he needed to keep this lady sweet because he asked me, quite nicely, "Keep her happy will you?"

So, I went and got on this horse and it went over backwards and thought I'd broken my neck.

I had been wearing a skull cap but it isn't much good when you are under half a tonne of beast. I had tried to carry on afterwards, because I didn't want David to see the pain I was in, which was excruciating.

Amazingly, I managed to drive home in my battered old Ford Granada that I'd bought for 60 quid at Pannal Market. The car had a red door, a blue door and a yellow door. But by the time I'd reached home I couldn't move, and my next-door neighbour had to come and rescue me and take me to hospital.

When I got to hospital they told me I had a fractured vertebrae and that I had pulled all the neck muscles and shoulder and shoulder blade muscles. I was told I'd never be able to ride again. There was even talk at one time of me never being able to walk again if the fracture had gone differently.

It had happened about Christmas time and I was worried about the progress of a horse that David and I had started working with. It was one that we had high hopes of doing well. Jockey Mark Birch came and rode him.

I was back at work with the collar on, but I was in agony. I was trying to prove that I deserved my wages, but I really was suffering.

And that was that. I left. I'd not even been with David for more than eight months. I'd had the best job in the world for me at the time, but because of this girl I'd nearly lost my life, I'd lost any career I'd hoped for and although David would have paid me for time off, I have always believed in working and didn't want to take money from him that I hadn't earned. I thought that was unfair, so I handed my notice in.

I was in hospital for 3 days and they sent me home all strapped up with this collar on. Fortunately, I found out that nearly everything was a muscular injury, that I hadn't broken my neck, but I had this chip in the vertebrae.

Home for me by then was in Raskelf. I'd got my own place. How that had come about had been that when we had come out of the kennels at Arkendale, which is where we were for the York & Ainsty South, we had a lovely house in Thirsk, on Racecourse Road.

I'd said I wasn't going to go with my father to his next role, and instead I made out that I had digs, as though I was paying rent somewhere. I wasn't. I just didn't want to be around at home.

Things were going wrong for my parents by then. My mother had become an alcoholic and my father was just very difficult to live with. They eventually split up.

For a short time, I was sleeping out of my Ford Granada while parked up at the aerodrome at Tholthorpe, well out of the way of human beings, which suited me just fine.

I'd go into the Old Black Bull in Raskelf to play pool. The lady in the post office in the village, Kath, knew my circumstances, that I'd been living out of my car and got me my first proper home of my own as she knew of a little place that was empty which cost me £15 per month.

I remember going to Calvert's Carpets and offering them a

tenner for all the offcuts of carpets out of the skip. Then I tied them to the roof of the car and brought them home and laid the carpets myself.

I went to a furniture sale in Stillington and bought a load of furniture for not much money either. I got a phone put in the house, but it was one of those coin phones like you get in telephone boxes and pubs so that I only paid for it when I needed it. My TV was a 50p television and I had an electric meter. I had a simple business attitude. If I couldn't pay for it, I couldn't have it.

Now let me tell you this tale. It happened after I had been taken on as a stable lad and when I was finding my feet.

You see, this book is all about my life and what I've gone through to get to who I am today as the Yorkshire Horseman.

There is plenty to come about all of what I'm doing today and things that will send you into another world at times, but these are the real stories that have happened along the way and this next part still brings back the events of what happened one night.

I'd taken up cattle droving at livestock markets. I'd started off at Pannal for the Robinsons who used to run it; and I was also a drover at Thirsk and Northallerton. Washing down the marts after the sales and droving during the sales was my job.

There's a photograph of me in this book at Boroughbridge Horse Fair where I would also show ponies for gypsies and I'd get a quid for running them up and down. My next job was a job on a maggot farm. I've worked for a butcher as well, but it was driving a wagon as a knackerman that kicked off this next story.

I'd pick everything up, making sure everything I was supposed to collect was done, but I'd see that some of the others had some scam going on. The yard manager must have been involved too because all of a sudden I started being threatened.

In the works canteen I was told that they were talking about putting me through the butchery's mincer. I took little notice. I wasn't scared of them.

The next day I had a day off. I was still at home with my parents at Thirsk. The yard manager came to our front door and said he wanted me to come down to the yard for a little talk.

I thought here we go.

I am not a violent man. I have never gone around looking for trouble and I have never ever been the instigator of a fight, but I am or at least I was, because I haven't had to resort to this since my twenties, someone who can defend himself.

And this is the key to what happens next. And to all you younger ones reading this. I didn't ask for this, I didn't intend it to happen, but I did stand up for myself against the bullies, just as I had done in the dinner queue at school years earlier.

This man had come to my house with one intention. It wasn't going to be pretty. You didn't need any heebie-jeebie stuff to work that one out. He wasn't asking to talk anything through. I would have been walking directly into an ambush.

What do you do in that situation?

Well in my case, it was to get in first. This guy underestimated me, like a lot of people have done over the years.

He'd walked up our garden path on Racecourse Road – and he went out the same way, well nearly, except this time he went backwards over the garden gate.

One punch, that's all it took. He never saw it coming, probably never expected it. It broke his nose. I got him by his windpipe. I hope he had a good dental plan arranged because my next blow knocked out his front row and the final one fractured his jaw. I might only have been nine-stone dripping wet through, but I had a six-pack on me. When you are with horses you have to learn how to look after yourself.

I got arrested for it, but he didn't press charges. He knew he stood no chance because he knew that everything else would be uncovered about what he and his mates were up to at work.

And that wasn't all.

Early on you will remember that I mentioned my siblings and that my brother Rodney ended up with a mental health problem and would go with the wrong 'uns to try and fit in. Keep that locked in for a second.

I'm out one night in Thirsk and my brother was too, with his so-called mates who were probably also a few slices short of a loaf. I was doing well in my work. I also had my own inner confidence and Rodney never got that.

I think he was always a bit jealous. I don't know whether he actually hated me at the time, and bless him he's gone now, but he certainly didn't have his head switched on right.

Maybe he'd had too many beers and had been easily led by his mates. I'd got home and was in the sitting room when Rodney comes through with his mates, one of whom was at least 6ft 3 and I'm thinking I've seen you somewhere before. This isn't going to end well, was my initial thought, more so for them but I wasn't over-confident. Father was oblivious to all this. He was in bed.

This wasn't something I initiated. I was just sitting here in my own home, minding my own business. Having a cuppa. They came in threatening me. In fact, I don't even remember them getting that far with any words. It was just their manner that told me they were about to attack me.

I'd already calculated what was happening, just as quickly as I had counted numbers on a blackboard as my teacher had been writing them on it years before. I knew what the result was going to be before my teacher had and I knew that my calculation had come up with 'fell the big lad first'.

I gave the lad the option. I don't think he was very good with understanding words. I said, "If you're brave enough, have a go." He kind of took a while for it to penetrate.

I saw the lad move slightly, but he was slow, too slow in thought and deed. His first move brought about my first blow, much more quickly and decisively than his. I climbed up this big lad like he was a ladder, swiftly broke his nose and jaw and split his head wide open by grabbing his ears and walloping it against the door. He was felled like a tree.

I rammed my brother's head into the door sneck. His other mate was in the corner. I ran upstairs. These guys were clearly not bothered about their future dental bill or health insurance claim. They were now totally committed to their target. Me.

My brother had got up the stairs. These other two finally got me pinned on the bed. I'd put up a good show, but they were relentless and I honestly then heard the words come out of my brother's mouth saying, "I'll hold him, you kick him to death."

That's when Dad appeared. He got Rodney from behind. He'd pulled out a metal bar from the wardrobe and had fair feathered him with it. He did the same with the big guy, whose teeth were now scattered around the room.

The third guy, the smallest, ended up bent double with broken ribs.

I was taken to Ripon police station for the second time, and this time it did go to court. I'd put all three of them into hospital, with a bit of help from my father.

I was up for grievous bodily harm. I had beaten them up. The police hadn't believed a lad of my size could have done it.

The Clerk of the Court asked whether I was pleading guilty

or not guilty. I barely stood high enough for the lady judge to see me. I said that I had kicked the living daylights out of them, but that I had only been protecting myself.

By that time, I had realised the other two that had been with my brother had been the guys that were going to put me through the mincer. Like I said, my brother Rodney had taken up with bad 'uns again, and they had used him.

The judge shook her head. I think she looked at me and them and thought, "Really? Is this the right way round here?" She told me to get myself on my way home and keep out of bad company. The three of them, including Rodney, all got bound over to keep the peace for two years.

I won't let people faze me, whoever they are, but like I keep saying, give me horses any day of the week.

CHAPTER 9

Early Signs of the Yorkshire Horseman: Clydesdales

After having given my notice to David Chapman I didn't get back into horses straight away, and anyway, I had been told I shouldn't ride, so I was no good as a stable lad any longer.

I had taken another driving job, this time for RK Furniture in Easingwold. They were specialists in office furniture, and I would be either off to London or Glasgow and all points in between, above and below. I drove for them for about six months and then left because they were short-staffed in the factory and had wanted me to work there.

I'd never worked in a factory in my life and I wasn't going to start. I told them I was either in the van or gone. And I went. I have always meant what I have said.

That took me back into horses. I had only been without them for a short while and I knew that I was still all about horses even though I'd been told not to be because of my neck, but I couldn't see any other way that I would want to live my life.

I'd also had ideas coming to me about how I could start something up.

What I had proven good at right since I'd been a little lad had been working with difficult horses. They had either been called dangerous, which was why they had come to the kennels for dog meat, or they had been suicide rides at the racehorse yards I'd worked in, but I'd done well with each and every one of them.

That girl at David's yard had been a supposed expert in breaking horses, but she clearly hadn't done her job well. I'd seen her at work and I'd also been her fall guy, a victim of her incompetence.

That's why I turned to breaking horses in. It felt right. It was another part of a horseman's life experience. I'd done it with tricky so-and-sos, I was sure I'd get more, but I'd also get some that were easier.

I could no longer take a stable lad's role anymore, but this was another part of my learning, another part that was to add to what would become the Yorkshire Horseman.

I'd seen an advertisement renting stables on Jenny Hunton's Nova Farm just out of Easingwold on the Stillington road. I'd rented one, as I'd been talking to a lady from near Thirsk who had Clydesdale stallions.

I'd only rented one stable, because that's what I'd been expecting, but she brought seven!

What a start! I went from one stable to seven in one go! My money was coming in straight away. I'd thought I would have to take on another job as well, but this really set me going.

This was also about the time that Barbara and I got together. I'd had my neck injury at David's and now had the Clydesdales, but I was still living at Raskelf, which is where we had met. Barbara used to live next door to the pub, the Old Black Bull, where I'd play pool.

Our relationship started and just grew. I'd never had a proper girlfriend until Barbara. We got married about five years later. Barbara doesn't like the publicity, so we'll leave it at that, but we have three great kids who I'll tell you more about later.

The lady with the Clydesdales didn't know me, but she knew of me. She'd heard I was good with tricky horses and knew these would probably prove a little difficult because they'd never been broken in before. They were big things as you'd expect with them being heavy horses, and might react against being broken in, a bit like the phrase, "You can't teach an old dog new tricks."

She had these majestic heavy horses to haul carts and wanted them breaking in so that she could sell as stallions that were handleable. They were all between four to eight years old and had not been broken before because she had been running them with her mares, using them as stud horses.

They did take quite a bit of time breaking in. Seven of them, all with their own temperaments, all having had lives that had been until then very carefree, nobody telling them what to do, just there to produce the next generations. It was like having a load of mature men who don't want to be told what to do, but I did a right job with them.

In fact, I went way over and above my job and I made them into proper horses that you could do anything with. They ended up being used for more than just hauling carts. And they were all true gentlemen by the time I'd finished with them. These gentle giants were the first of what was to become a really great and important step in my equine career.

That's right. I now had an equine career. I felt I'd reached another milestone and for the first time in my life I was being taken seriously in a business that was wholly mine – and with horses!

Those seven Clydesdales were my own Magnificent Seven – and they really were magnificent. Working with them for the four months I had them was a very real pleasure. I fetched on all of my experience of working with those horses that were to be shot, for the good of these seven Clydesdales and made them good horses.

Before I took them on, I had been thinking that I hadn't been getting a lot out of life, but having them and concentrating on them, understanding their needs and bringing them to the point at which the lady from Thirsk wanted them to reach, brought me all of the pleasure and satisfaction in the world.

While I had the Clydesdales, I also had other people come to me.

I had a girl who lived just up the lane who I was talking with one day, just in normal, "How are you?" conversation, but I could tell she was really upset. She told me her horse was lame and that the vet had said they couldn't do anything and so she was going to have him put down.

I'd seen it in the field from the road with one of the Clydesdales I'd broken. I looked closer and said the problem was a foreign body just above the foot in the coronet band. I told her there was something like a splinter or a thorn.

I said that her vet should be able to sort that out, but that I had a way of drawing it out if she wanted to try.

When she'd asked me to, I asked her to go to the local shop and get me the biggest cabbage she could find, and I also asked if she had some bandages.

At first, I think she just wondered what was going on. Was I a bit strange, perhaps? But she was giving it a go, for the cost of a cabbage.

I told her that the cabbage leaves were going to draw out the foreign bodies. I could tell she was still unsure, but like I said it was only costing her a cabbage. I wrapped the horse's leg and coronet in cabbage leaves, then I bandaged it.

It's a fact that cabbage leaves sweat and in so doing they, plus the heat built up by putting on the bandage, draw out what is under layers of skin.

The next day we took the bandages off, she came back and there was a splinter of wood a quarter of an inch long in the cabbage leaf.

I said, "There you go, he'll be sound now," and he was. This girl still couldn't believe it, but although it was simple enough to think of an easy solution, even I still hadn't known for definite it would work.

That information I'd received about the foreign body was either coming from the animal, the way it was uncomfortable in its movement or the spirit guide that was working with me to help.

Either way, I just went along with the information I had received. This was perhaps, and unknown to me at the time, the start of how my life was going to be.

I knew I wasn't destined to ride a winner at the Cheltenham Festival, I wasn't destined to be riding at the Horse of the Year Show, but for me I now had something much more special in my life.

I'd always known I could work with horses right from saving all those horses from Death Row, but now I was actually doing so as my work, my business and my career.

I was no longer the yard sweeper, the excrement shoveller, someone to be looked down on. I no longer had to hear all, see all and say nowt – now, what I said had started to matter and people wanted to hear me.

But for me it was and still is all about helping horses – first, foremost and last. Horses can't help themselves. They need someone to understand them and to be able to find out what makes them contented and happy in whatever they are going to do in their lives.

There is a philosophy that if a horse is put in a field it has to stay there, or if it is put in a stable then it must stay there the same, but some horses, like people, don't want to stay in there and owners don't understand that. Some horse owners only see the horse, they see four legs and a head. What they don't see is the heart and soul inside.

It's all about understanding not just what is best for the horse but about getting to know what it likes doing, where it likes to be. And that is all about tuning in to them.

While I was breaking the Clydesdale stallions I thought about upping the ante, charging a bit more for breaking in horses, because I knew that I wasn't charging enough for the time I was putting in – and also because this was what I really, truly wanted to do and was where I wanted to be. I was enjoying working purely for myself, not for anyone else.

I decided that my independence, running my own equine business, not being told what to do by others, was more important to me than the money.

So, to build up the income, instead of spoiling my horsebreaking business by overpricing it, I bought a little eight-seater minibus rather than having a car, which I could use as my transport to the stables as well as using it to ferry people about.

The buses were there to help me keep going with the breaking, but soon I found that business was taking off too!

I was running around darts teams from pub to pub during the week and Easingwold Young Farmers Club started using me as well for their meetings, so I was out most Friday and Saturday nights – and my horse yard was about to grow massively too.

It was great. My income was growing. What I was doing with the horses was work I enjoyed doing, plus I'd made a new income through the minibus that contributed to the equine business.

For me, working with horses has never been about money. It has always been about feeling good in myself, feeling at ease with myself, a feeling of satisfaction that I'm doing what I am meant to be doing. Believe me, there is nothing better than being able to fulfil your dream and make it work for you.

We all get knocks in our lives, but here I was working on my dream. All I can tell you is whatever your dream is, pursue it, because when it comes you will know true happiness.

People see it in you too. They see you bloom. They see your shoulders back rather than rounded shoulders carrying the world.

I was a new person. I was what people like to call 'pumped'. I was doing not just the job I loved, working with horses, but I was also getting paid to do it. There is nothing better than being able to make what you love doing into something that also works for you. And I was now really earning a reputation.

And building up a reputation and a demand meant I needed bigger premises, more stables. That's when I moved to a bigger yard at Helperby through a great man called David Faulkner who let me have this yard at Brafferton Hall.

David really looked after me and both he and David Chapman restored some of my faith in people who owned things. I had now moved up rapidly from having seven horses stabled to stabling for 28. I had all the stables filled within eight months.

David knew where I was coming from and because I'd worked with his good friend David Chapman there was already a good connection. David (Chapman) had spoken very highly of me to him.

That's when Ruth's Gamble came to me, but was unnamed at the time. I was to be working with my first racehorse. Another important moment for me, another real milestone for this lad that had grown up being thought of as an insignificant misfit. I was finally making my mark. It was a great feeling.

David sent me this young horse to see what I could do with it. He sent me three, but Ruth's Gamble was the one that was to be my first racing success and it was David's first winner as a two-year-old.

I told David that he had an amazing horse, but that he shouldn't rush me, that the horse would turn out right. It just needed the right time. David kept pushing me. He'd bred the horse and was itching to see it run. He knew it would do well, but that it just needed careful handling beforehand.

When I knew that Ruth's Gamble was ready, I called David and said, "I've got some good news for you, sir." Like I said earlier, I've always called him "sir" and I always called his wife Marion, "madam". They respected me and I respected both of them.

I said, "Your horse can come back on one condition that when it comes back I come and ride it every day for first week to ten days to get it settled in, because this truly will be a great racehorse." That's exactly what happened.

David told me one day, a short while later, "I've some good news for you. Ruth's Gamble runs at Musselburgh on Saturday. I said, "I'll tell you now, sir, he'll win." I knew he would win – and he did, but not at Musselburgh where he finished third in his first outing. He won five days later, by four lengths, in a field of 13 at Doncaster. David's first win with a two-year-old in his training career. I was buzzing! So was David!

Ruth's Gamble went on to win eight times in its career over hurdles and on the flat. What a horse! And I had played my part. It proves that if you give a young horse time to learn and grow in confidence, its ability will follow.

I had another that David sent too. I can't for the life of me remember his name. David ran him at Market Rasen and he also went and won. I was on Cloud Nine.

Others didn't know any of this but I didn't really care. Once again I knew I was partly responsible for another racehorse success. It won five consecutive races.

When David and I talked years later about what had happened at the time that I'd given in my notice, I'd reiterated just how much I was truly grateful to him and how he had set an example for me. That I appreciated everything he had done and how he had shown me great kindness

It was then that I said the reason why I had left his employ was that I had thought it was unfair of me to take money off him and not work.

That's when David said it would have been alright because the government would have been paying him to do that. I hadn't known. I hadn't needed to leave and, had I known that, I probably wouldn't have handed my notice in and would still have been working there – but then I wouldn't have started my own business breaking horses! It's a funny old world.

My horsebreaking business continued to grow, but it will always be David Chapman who helped me more than anyone before or since and gave me that confidence to believe in myself.

David Chapman was a great believer in what I believe in, that there is a key somewhere to make every horse click.

CHAPTER 10

Giving Horses a Life:
Duster & the Young Pretender

As well as being a horseman, with all my years of experience in working with horses, whether breaking, rehabilitating, training as racehorses or simply getting them right for those who just want to hack, I also have this spiritual side.

Some call me a medium, others a psychic, clairvoyant, spiritualist or clairsentient. I may be all of those. All I do know is that I can help horses because of the expertise I have developed through working with them; and through this other world.

I cannot properly define it and I'm not bothered about doing so. I do like the term clairsentient because that is described as having the most down-to-earth status of the lot, even though I don't mind the other terms. They are all what set me apart from others and have made my name.

Clairsentient is when you have clear, intuitive feelings about things and people and animals. For me that comes over as feeling the horse's emotions. Who knows where all this comes from? A better man or woman will be able to tell you. All I can say for sure is that this all started with the stag when I was three or four years old.

It is that clairsentience that I receive intuitively, without having to think at all about it, that combined with my horsemanship, has always been able to help.

Now I'd like to share with you two quite different but very important stories to me that both took place in the 1990s.

First, the story of Duster.

Duster was a hunt horse, a grey. Harry Stephenson, who I'd known from being a young boy, had him and said Duster was knackered and asked if I had room for him. I took him in and found him a new owner called Marion who was quite happy with him being here in my stables. She would feed him and got pleasure from having him.

We found out that Duster was 31 years old. No wonder he was knackered, but my clairsentience kicked in telling me that he wanted to go hunting again. I'd felt it when I was sitting on him and I could feel the sadness when I looked into his eyes. He was an old man, but he still longed for what he had done most of his life. I was feeling that emotion coming out of him.

That's when I decided I would take him with the Bilsdale Hunt. I was busy with my buses, but I took him because I wanted to please him. I wanted him to feel good about himself. That day, at the hunt, he was like a five-year-old.

I could feel a young horse, his heart, the ambition. He'd got back all these feelings from his youth and I felt good too. It was like 'phwoar' we're back on the job.

What man, what horseman in his right mind, would take a 31-year-old horse out hunting? Nobody would, not even me.

I didn't jump him. He was far too old for that. He ran with the hunt, but I took him through the gates. I could feel he was living on his memories. He'd had a good career. We had three hours together. He'd been around all of the other horses at the meet, but from then on it had been just me and Duster.

Duster came back home that day and he looked fantastic. His ears were pricked. I knew he was feeling good.

Two weeks later Duster lay down and died. What I had been getting through his messages and my clairsentience were his last wishes. I am so glad that I was driven to do what we did that day at Bilsdale because I know that Duster died a happy horse.

Second up, the amazing but true story of The Young Pretender.

Local knackerman Harry Atkinson asked me to go over to near Bridlington to pick up a horse. He'd been told it was supposed to be destroyed, but Harry had said to take it back to mine and see what I could make of it.

So I go over and this feller says, "Aye lad, it's down in t'field, if you can catch it. It's 'ell of a big thing, all of 17.3 'ands." He said this as he looked at me, nine stone wet through. The horse was a proper Irish Draught.

Harry rang me the next day and said, "Have you got the horse?" I said, "Yeah, it took a bit of catching."

He said, "See if you can break him in, he's never been handled." I said, "He has, because he wouldn't be as clever if someone hadn't had a go at him, he's too cute."

So, I started on him, broke him in and started riding him. Several weeks later I took him to show Harry at his home in Thorpe Bassett, because Harry was ill.

I told Harry I'd been able to do all sorts with him. Now, Harry was always a man who saw opportunity and he said, "There's a high-performance sale at Royal Ascot. We'll have that horse there."

This horse had been stuck in a field a few weeks previously, nobody wanted to touch it, it was to be put down.

For all children reading and for those who can't stomach certain language, I won't say exactly what I said. Here's a slightly different version. I said, "Fettling hell, Harry!" But he just said,

Pretty well dressed
for me at 14 years old
with my mum Mary.

My dad Tom with the Atherstone Hunt.

Dad at the Derwent Point-to-Point.

My grandma Olive Garcia.

My sister Charlotte on Timmy, the pony I bought for £25 and sold for £360 when I was nowt but a lad.

Going to the start at Charm Park Point-to-Point in 1976 on Mrs Blue (another milkman's horse!) with Dad alongside me.

At Boroughbridge Horse Fair when in my early 20s.

Duster's final ride at Bilsdale Hunt, not bad for a horse of over 30 years old. We had a great day.

The Young Pretender at Thorpe Bassett – Harry Atkinson and I took him to a High Performance Show & Sale at Ascot where this allegedly wild horse went from being worth nothing to a lot of money in just a few weeks.

Racehorse trainer days with jockey Declan McGann when Sylvie D'Orthe ran at Sedgefield.

Schooling my racehorse North at Fawdington.

A young Alex listening in to my instructions to our jockey riding River Trapper at Sheriff Hutton.

If you can't beat them, join them – or become one of them. I was the pony for a wedding at Linton-on-Ouse for one of my Young Farmers Club friends.

North leading the way at Musselburgh.

In action at one of my evenings where I raise funds for Riding for the Disabled.

Working with horses and bringing them back to life is what I do.

Royal MacNab enjoying his retirement.

Teapot & Millie – two lovely horses in rehabilitation.

"No, we'll have it. I'll get a wagon and you can go down with him." And off we went.

When I got there, he'd entered me and our young pretender in a dressage class! This monster of a horse only tamed a few weeks back, hardly ever ridden. And me, master of the dressage? I'd never even done it before!

I went, "FFS (I believe that is an expression people use today) Harry! I wouldn't have a clue how to do that!"

That wasn't all. He said, "I've entered you in a jumping competition as well." I asked what he'd entered me in? He said 130 (that's 130cm-high fences). I said, "Fettle me! He can't jump 50 centimetres! Pull him out of that one. I'll go in the dressage and walk about a bit."

So that's what I did. I walked about and trotted him in circles. I came out from the dressage and he'd still got me in jumping as well! He might have jumped three foot at the most before, but these fettling things were nearly four foot.

In the end Harry relented. "Well, don't go in then," he said.

And how he'd behaved and performed in the dressage proved enough because he made £7,800! That was in the 90s and is probably equivalent to £20,000 today. The new owners bought him because they could see the quality in him.

Harry was a lovely character and was pleased with himself and knew I'd done all the graft.

He said, "Done alright with that horse, didn't we?" I said, "Aye, Harry, we did, but he was hard work." He said, "I'm not surprised, nobody else could break him."

We never gave him a name. He was six years old when we had him, and I've always known him as The Young Pretender.

What happened between myself and The Young Pretender was all down to my horsemanship, no particular clairsentience, no spiritual stuff, just honest to goodness horsemanship.

The Young Pretender, we'll give him his name properly now, had been a horse that somebody had had a go with and the horse had got the better of him or her. And he was a wise horse.

I used my skillset. To get him out of a 20-acre field on to a wagon is not an easy task and I still don't know how I did it, but I did.

The way I look at it is this. If you create an argument, you're going to create unease. I never had an argument with that horse. I was there to help him and he followed me up the field and through the gate and into the yard and then I walked him into the fold yard. I backed my wagon up to the gate, I dropped the ramp, showed him it and he just walked in.

It's easy when you know how.

CHAPTER 11

The Racehorse Trainer:
In the Making

Those days of working with David's racehorses had given me a real confidence boost. I now knew that I had something in me that extended way beyond just putting difficult horses right. I now had this growing reputation for helping prepare racehorses. And my next move was to take me even nearer to another goal of being a bona fide racehorse trainer.

There was this garage owner, Peter Nelson in Helperby, who had been repairing my old, knackered cars. I'd buy one on the cheap nearly every six months for not much money, but they always needed work doing to them and it was Peter who had kept me on the road until I got into minibuses.

Peter had a racehorse in training called Magic Bloom and it wasn't doing any good for him. The horse had been entered in 11 races and had pulled up or been at the back of the field in all but one.

There was something definitely not right with this horse and I kept telling Peter to take it out of this yard in Doncaster and bring it to me at Brafferton Hall. I told him I would freshen it up a bit and we could make a plan for the horse. In the end Peter decided to do just that.

Peter was so proud of Magic Bloom but his knowledge of horses was not there and whatever the previous trainer had told

Peter he'd believed. It is understandable. Peter had gone into racehorse ownership, like many before him, because he liked the races, the atmosphere, not because he knew about horses. He knew about cars.

Well, I'm not kidding you, when Magic Bloom came off the wagon and into my place, I could not believe what I was seeing. There was no bloom, not even a wilting. This horse was close to dying.

I said to Peter, "My God, what is that?!" It was like something being dropped off by the RSPCA. This was supposed to be a racehorse. It was unreal.

Magic Bloom wasn't looking very magic at all. She was just skin and bone and had all sorts of boils and blemishes. What a mess. She was about six or seven years old and if I had been her previous trainer, I would have been ashamed to say that I'd looked after her.

My immediate reaction to Peter was to tell him that we needed a vet to this horse. I said, "It's nearly emaciated. We need the vet out to do its teeth so it can eat and digest properly." Her teeth were sharp, it needed a wormer, it was desperate for a B12 vitamin jab to give it a boost. I said, "Let's get the vet in first, then leave the rest to me. Don't let anybody tell me or you what to do. I will get a proper racehorse out of this horse for you."

David Faulkner, who I was renting the stables from, had a big interest in Magic Bloom and could not believe that I could turn the horse's form around and he said so.

But for me there was something about this horse, for all of its preference for pulling up in races up to that point and despite its near emaciation. Something was telling me it was a good 'un and well worth the time.

In my head, spiritually, I was hearing these words, "If I can't get that to win a race, I'll retire."

I told Mr Faulkner that things aren't always about what is said on the tin and that none of us should be over-influenced by what we see or read. To be fair to David he then said he'd found what I said very interesting.

I worked away solidly with this horse for months. It was back fit and looked every inch the racehorse it should have done.

And boy was Magic Bloom fit. And also, what a character. I was preparing a racehorse that was to go on to win nine times in her career, but up to this point had been just like the milk horses I'd had when I was a point-to-point jockey. This horse was made to run!

And boy this horse would fly!

Once I'd got Magic Bloom going again there was no stopping her. And she wasn't too concerned about having me on board, that's for sure. Four times Magic Bloom decided she didn't need me, and I was deposited each time, taking the bridle with me too.

When it happened the first time, I was quick to get in touch with Peter who came to me. We looked everywhere and couldn't find her. She had disappeared.

Not for one moment had either of us thought about the possibility it would go home until David Faulkner joined us, asking what we were looking for. I told him what had happened and he said, "That black mare? I've just shut the door on her. She's in the stable. I wondered where you were."

From then on every time Magic Bloom decided I was unnecessary baggage I just went home and there she was.

It was at this stage I said to Peter that we were now at the time where we either stopped working with her, in case she was getting too much of a handful, or we put her properly back in training, because that hadn't been my role. Mine had been getting her back right, back at full strength, fit and raring to go.

I said she needed to be somewhere where she needed the right handling. She was, as I now knew, a very quirky, talented horse. She was different and there was a unique key to get the best out of her. I knew she had reached the point where she needed a trainer that would understand and respond to her mood. I would have loved to take her on myself, but I didn't have a trainer's licence.

Magic Bloom was sent to a trainer who we will call Nobby Smith. I went with Peter. I knew that Magic Bloom needed to run and said he needed to put it on his books and get her running very soon otherwise she would start going backwards. I'd spent the time with her. I knew the opportunity was there for the taking.

He didn't.

I told Nobby that he had to keep her right. She was all wound up and ready to go, but she needed to relax beforehand. I knew what she needed and how to get the best out of her.

After he'd had her a short time I wasn't happy with how he was working her. He didn't want to listen to me.

It was when he said, "If you're so clever ride it out yourself," that I took a hand and went over to his yard and rode her out every day. I did things that you would not normally do with a racehorse. I did the opposite.

I didn't want her worked, I just wanted her enjoying life. She was ready to race and I knew by now what her behaviour meant at each time and mood. I was listening to her body language, so sometimes I took her for a walk and sometimes I'd ride.

That's why I knew she was ready, but wouldn't be ready forever. You had to really read this horse. After about a month to six weeks of going to Nobby's yard I couldn't contain myself any longer.

I had come back from another session and had just turned her into the paddock. I'd said it was time he had Magic Bloom entered into a race.

Nobby was very sarcastic and said, "Oh right, Mr Trainer now are we? What do you want me to do, run it in the Gold Cup?"

To my mind he was just taking his £200 a week stable and training fees. He didn't seem to give two hoots about the horse.

I was doing this all for nothing because I had absolute faith this horse was going to win more than one race. I told him that if he wasn't going to run her, to send her home.

In the end he gave in and entered Magic Bloom in a race at Newcastle over hurdles. That's when I then did a piece of work with Nobby on another horse on the gallops.

He was on this horse Mr Chips that had won at the Ebor meeting in York. A flat racing horse that went like the wind. I was on Magic Bloom. My goodness we were travelling.

I looked over my shoulder and Nobby was a good three lengths down, giving it some, but Magic Bloom was flying. When I pulled her up and Nobby joined me he said, "You got a length on me there." I said that it had been far more than that. Nobby didn't speak to me after that until just before Magic Bloom's first race with him as trainer. Trainer? What a joke!

On the day, Nobby said, "Right, Mr Trainer, what's the orders for the jockey?"

I said, "A bucket full."

I said to get the jockey to sit her in tight on the rail, have her there or thereabouts, turn her wide on the home turn, give her two smacks and she would be gone, that she would romp home.

I watched the whole race. I saw Magic Bloom turn for home and Nobby must have told the jockey, even though he had sulked when I'd told him. The jockey sat there, had her handy and whoosh, Magic Bloom did exactly as I had predicted. She sailed home. I was in tears of joy. I'd waited about fourteen months to prove my point.

The following day Peter was having a party. He was understandably over the moon. I'd been invited and so had 'the trainer', the man who hadn't wanted to run Magic Bloom, and Nobby was taking all the credit.

Like I have said before, I'd never really been given any praise, and while it really didn't matter to me too much because I knew what I had done with this horse, what happened next was a special moment for me and another indication of the regard with which I was starting to be held.

David Faulkner got up and said, "I'd just like to say if it hadn't been for Cooper Wilson, Magic Bloom would never have run again."

I really appreciated David's words.

Nobby hardly ever spoke to me again, except when he felt it was absolutely necessary, when he needed me just before a race.

A fortnight later at Wetherby I told him to tell the jockey to do just the same as at Newcastle. Magic Bloom won again beating what had been regarded as a really good horse that went on to win at Cheltenham.

Nobby was getting all the plaudits.

Magic Bloom's next race was at Market Rasen and I told Nobby I would run her as front runner there. I knew what the horse was comfortable with and I had known that Newcastle and Wetherby are very similar galloping tracks, but that Market Rasen isn't because you are on the bend more of the time.

I told Nobby she would be comfortable and relaxed at the front. The one thing to keep Magic Bloom right was to make sure she did not stress. Like us as human beings, we run better when we are relaxed rather than riled up.

It really is all about understanding the horse.

This time he took no notice. He knew best because she had won twice the same way, and in his head she would do so again and again. She didn't. She finished fourth. He had proved himself not to listen. After that I never went back to his yard because he obviously wasn't going to listen any longer and her form went, she became useless for him.

When Peter asked what was going wrong I told him that Nobby wouldn't listen to me and that he (Peter) should consider moving Magic Bloom to someone else. It took a while, but we got her to Malcolm Jefferson's yard – and Magic Bloom bloomed again, but it took a while.

I was up at Kelso two years later in 1995 with another horse and Malcolm was there when I went into the canteen. I asked how Magic Bloom was doing. Malcolm said, "I just don't know. I don't know what you did to get that horse to win." We had a cup of tea and I told him about my methodology, how I had dealt with Magic Bloom's ways. Malcolm said he found it very hard to believe that I had managed it.

Malcolm had worked for the great Gordon Richards. He had been his travelling head lad and then head lad. He knew his job inside out and was a cracking trainer and horseman. It was perhaps going to be difficult for him to take on something new from a young man like me.

Now, I've never known whether Malcolm did what I said but that mare then went on and won four races from June to September 1995, so I have an inkling that Malcolm did go back and try some of what I said to get the best out of the horse.

A lot of people think a good horse is one that is easy to train, but believe you me a good horse can be very hard to train.

There are many who think that successful racehorse trainers like Martin Pipe and Paul Nicholls find it easy because they are buying the best horses, but that's not true. They are successful because of the hours they put in and how they train, how they work. Attention to detail, just like Nicky Henderson.

Bringing the best out of Magic Bloom was all about understanding her mindset and a lot of people couldn't work her out. Everyone thought she couldn't do intensive training. I had worked out that, rather like some footballers, it was just that she didn't need it. Now that was what Malcolm found difficult to understand too, and I totally got that, but it was right. She didn't.

It's the psyche thing that I have, that ability to understand the horse's needs that made all the difference. Nobby was never going to listen. He wasn't open to something different. But Malcolm, while also not quite believing what I had done, was a trainer who didn't discount anything. And Magic Bloom bloomed again.

CHAPTER 12

The Racehorse Trainer

Because of my successes with Ruth's Gamble, Magic Bloom and other horses, I kind of fancied having a go at becoming a licenced trainer and had the confidence and belief in myself, but I also needed to keep the money coming in to make sure I could afford some horses and so the period from 1994 to 1997 saw me getting busier everywhere.

I'd moved from David Faulkner's place at Brafferton Hall to Fawdington Lodge, part of the Helperby Estate. I rented it through David and had ten stables built there to pursue my racehorse trainer ambitions and to provide stabling for the horsebreaking.

The bus business, which had been there to help provide additional revenue over and above what the horsebreaking was bringing in, had now become the main earner.

That hadn't been the general idea, but once you've got money coming in you want to keep it coming. And although I never wanted to run any kind of business other than being with my horses, having the buses was paying for buying racehorses and keeping them.

In order to achieve my ambition to get my ticket and become a licenced racehorse trainer I first had to become an assistant trainer.

I'd met Gerry Kelly at David Chapman's yard. He was a

lovely man who'd help anybody and I asked whether he would put me on as assistant trainer. That's how I became assistant trainer to Gerry at the yard he rented in Sheriff Hutton. He was also known as GP Kelly and, like me, had become known for what some writers had called "a lifetime of riding the bad, dangerous and downright lunatic horses."

Gerry had three winners while I was working with him. He was a lovely feller, a proper Irishman and helped me get my trainer's permit.

I was with Gerry as assistant trainer and had to go to the Northern Racing School at Doncaster and then to Newmarket for a week to study for an NVQ in Horse Management.

I was now working every hour known to man and having started with just one minibus within six years I had seven coaches running. I was driving one of the buses and I had six other drivers including my sister Charlotte.

My biggest bus was a 32-seater. I also had two 16-seaters; and three 26-seaters and the original minibus. I had picked up school-run contracts and the whole thing had really taken off, but there was no room anywhere to take a break, especially after I took on my racehorse trainer's permit in 1996.

My normal day went like this. I would get up at four in the morning, take a couple of the horses that were in training out to the gallops and after that I'd go and drive the school bus. Then I'd come back and take another horse out. After that I would work on the horses I was breaking in for others and after that I would be back on the afternoon school runs, often more than one per day. And there were a load of other jobs that also needed sorting.

The horses I had in training were all mine. I'd have two or three at a time and in my early days I had Cottonon, Kilmond

Wood and Shildon as well as Marsh's Law that I'd had with Gerry; and Kilmond Wood was my first runner having gained my permit.

I trained racehorses right through until 2008. I had a great time, but I couldn't afford the investment in really good horses. I was getting so much out of doing the best I could with what I had, and of course I would have loved to have winners, who wouldn't, but I was realistic and knew that I was giving them my best.

The way I trained them, because they were horses at the end of their career, or should never have been racehorses in the first place, they gave the best they could.

Racehorse training isn't all about the trainers who have hundreds of winners, there are hundreds and thousands more who aren't up there with what people regard as the best, but they understand their horses just as much as those who have had the winners. Those who've had all the winners, the ones who I really respect, will tell you the same.

I wasn't working with anything destined to be Champion Hurdle, Gold Cup or Grand National winner – unless the rest of the field had fallen at somewhere like The Chair – but I was like a lot of other trainers who didn't have the money to invest in the right ones and nor did I have people sending me any.

I was Cooper Wilson, the little lad that had come from a hunt servant's life, the 5ft 2 lad with the jug ears who nobody had wanted to be near, the lad that nobody wanted to talk to – but I had my horses, I was a trainer, I was living the dream, as they say.

Winning races wasn't what mattered most to me. I would have loved it, but I knew the horses I had and I knew their capabilities. What I did with them was to get their heart back into it or set them up to perform as well as they could.

If I'd had the money to buy a good one I would probably have been more successful, but I was working largely with broken horses.

Cottonon was a point-to-pointer, but she was a real hunting horse. I couldn't take her to the gallops, she just wouldn't go, so I used to hunt her three times a week with two stone of lead on to get her fit, because I was only 9st 6lbs.

Jockey Richard Whitaker rode her and she was running a cracking race at Cottingham, near Huntington. She jumped in second, two jumps out and was tracking a horse called 57 Channels when she burst a valve to her heart.

Kilmond Wood was ten years old when I bought him in 1995. He'd had his day. He'd won at Perth, Cartmel & Hexham six years previously. I'd bought him thinking hopefully he'd do something because he looked a good sort, but he had a wind problem. He ran at Doncaster. Peter Atkinson rode him and he fell at the first. No bother. That happens.

Then we ran him at Sedgefield and he started swallowing his tongue and couldn't get his wind. Peter was jockey again and pulled him up. They'd just started the wind operation then and back in the day they used to open them up, now it's done by laser. The operation wasn't successful.

I didn't think it was fair to keep putting him through it. He'd had a great racing life and it was time for him to enjoy the rest of it, so I sold him to a woman over near Withernsea. He only died in 2017–18, living until a grand old age of around 33. The lady used him as a hacker. I'd delivered him to her and she kept in touch.

Shildon was an eight-year-old Irish horse I had bought for £1,500, all my life savings, at the Doncaster sales. He was the last horse in the sale and I had to have him otherwise I would be going home with nothing – and he had been useless.

I remember the wife playing hell with me, something along the lines of what was I wasting money on buying these no-hopers.

I said it was the only way I could get an education. I know a lot of others in the racing world would find my runners hilarious because I was only running what was termed the yak, but what they didn't realise was that I was actually learning valuable lessons.

Everyone in the racing world has a role and mine, given my lack of funds to do anything more, was to try and get the bad horses to run well, just as I'd been doing all my life, turning horses around.

Shildon was headstrong, but from the runs I got out of him you could see he had changed his mindset and his talent was coming through. I had a local lad, Ashley Bonson, on him at Charm Park twice.

But this yak had more within him.

The first time Ashley rode him there, he was going to hunt him around, but Shildon decided differently and gave it a good shot, going to the front and eventually finishing sixth, next time he finished fourth. We took him to Wetherby and by then we had decided he was a front runner where he settled better.

Shildon outjumped the horse that was alongside him at the front and put him on the floor; coming up to the last fence on the home straight he had been well in front when the now loose horse that had been alongside him pushed him out of the wing – and that was the end of that.

He had another point-to-point where he fell at Easingwold and then his final race was at Market Rasen where he pulled up with an injury to his leg with jockey Wayne Burnell on board.

It wasn't all doom and gloom at all. Racing for me isn't about that. It really is about enjoying it, hopefully doing well out of it and you can do well by achieving the best you can with each horse you have.

You can't make a silk purse out of a sow's ear – and you can't make a classic winning racehorse out of a milk horse, but you can make horses better, give them more confidence and build on their ability.

It might never be enough to turn them into something special, but you'll have done something special if they perform over and above what is expected – and other trainers respect that.

Shildon had given me some pleasure because he had run better than he had previously. We'd had a moment where he'd looked every inch the racehorse. These are the things you have to look back on with pride.

You see not everything is weighed in trophies and money – although it helps!

All these horses I ever had in training weren't generally easy to work with, but they improved my skills for what I do today. That's why I believe that when I was a trainer, I really was successful even without the winners.

When you watch racing it's alright watching the horse at the front winning, but if you watch down the field and you see the horses putting heart and soul into it, I still class them as good horses, they are all trying their best at that time.

When I had my license, every single horse I had was a broken horse from somewhere else. This is why I knew that I did well as a racehorse trainer in my own way. Obviously not in the public eye or with results in *Racing Post*, but my horses went out there and showed me you can rebuild trust in a horse by doing the right things.

Lots of people want to be successful and there are those who want to buy readymade success without putting the work in. I was always prepared to put in the hours, and I still do.

Marsh's Law was a real favourite of mine and you'll see why in these coming pages. He'd already had his good years, winning six races; three times at Market Rasen, and once each at Towcester, Hunstanton and Fakenham.

He was my horse that I ran as assistant to Gerry Kelly and he proved very important to me personally because of what happened not long after he had run his first race for me at Kelso in October 1997. He ran a great race and finished fourth.

It was around this time that I had everything going on. My breaking of horses was still proving popular; I was that busy with Country Travel, my bus business, which was running me ragged; and also trying my best to train my horses as well as I could. I never felt I had them as fit as I could have. It was the time factor that was the thing – I didn't have any!

In the end something had to give – and it did. And it was me that gave. I had a stroke.

CHAPTER 13

The Racehorse That Healed Me

My stroke was very mild. I was driving a bus when I felt it happening. You don't know what it is exactly, and I certainly had no idea it was a stroke I was having. I was only 36 years old and the thought of it didn't enter my head at first, and that I was just unwell.

I kept going, kept driving. I got everybody home. I was holding my arm, but I tried not to show that I was ill.

This is my brand of loyalty. I never feel the need to prove myself to anyone, but I have to do right by everybody.

I wasn't a danger to other road users. I drove slowly enough. I knew I wasn't right, but just said I was tired when anyone asked.

After the last passengers had got off, I drove home. I went to bed. Barbara took me off to our local GP the next day who sent me straight into York Hospital saying that I should have gone the previous night. I slept for three days, not that I really knew that at the time. They were all getting really worried.

But being in hospital was probably the best thing that could have happened to me.

I don't mean the stroke was the best thing of course, nor did the act of taking up a hospital bed appeal to me, but it just slowed me down, you see.

I'd been going at about a hundred miles an hour with everything I had on. It wasn't just the racehorses, the horsebreaking and the buses either, although that would have been enough. We had moved to Fawdington Lodge and we were expecting our first child, as Barbara was pregnant with Alex.

I'd never planned on being in charge of any type of company, let alone a bus company, and the stress of it all, just the running around here, there and everywhere had obviously taken its toll.

The stroke had come about because of what I was trying to achieve with the buses, the horses and trying to achieve my trainer's licence and that urge to work with racehorses probably over-rode everything else.

To me, the quality of life you can have for yourself is the most important thing, and trying to keep your family comfortable.

I was always driven to work with horses first and foremost. Even when I drove the buses I would always put someone else on a job and go and see a horse, because that horse can't speak for itself and some people can't understand the body language.

Now, although I couldn't be with horses in hospital, there are a number of things you can do when you are laid up in a hospital bed. You can rest up and recharge, allow yourself to get better, or you can run too fast and blow yourself out again within seconds of coming back, or you can give up.

I will admit there was a moment when I was still weak from the stroke and thought everything had gone and that I wouldn't be able to do what I had done before.

But on the other side of my head there was that something saying, "I can", and they are very important words. I knew right there and then. I said to myself "I can" and at that moment everything started to become clearer.

Being in hospital gave me the opportunity to reflect, to see how far I had come. I realised how proud I should be of what I had achieved with horses and the powers I possessed of being able to help and make the best out of them and how this scrawny youth had somehow, without any real school education and certainly no school qualifications, somehow become a business owner.

That's why when I was laid up I knew that "I can" was so important. It's what I had been doing all my life and I just knew that "I can" meant that I could and I would always survive and that I would always be successful, in my own way.

Me and horses, okay buses too, but it was always about me and horses.

And it was particularly special for me that it was a horse that got me back to full fitness. When I left hospital I was told by the doctors that I had to do nothing. I wasn't allowed to drive for six months anyway, so that ruled out any of my bus and coach work. Guess what that left me with? Horses, of course.

And I had Marsh's Law in the fields!

I used to ride him every day. I had decided I could ride him. I could trust him. When my doctor visited and saw me on him, she said I would get killed if I had another stroke and fell off the horse. I said, "At least I'll die happy!"

There's a saying that what's good for the inside of a man is the outside of a horse. He got me back fit. My consultant said he couldn't understand how I could go from so poorly to so well in such a short time.

It was all down to Marsh's Law and all of the horses I had worked with before him. Without having helped all of these horses previously I wouldn't have been in the position to know how much a horse could truly help me.

I became trainer as well as owner of Marsh's Law in March 1999 and he ran in a point-to-point at Dalton Park. Jockey Clive Mulhall rode him there and rode him brilliantly. Marsh's

Law always ran well and with Clive on board we had a really great team.

Clive's a racehorse trainer in his own right these days at Scarcroft, near Leeds, and he's won a few races. He understands horses and how to get the best out of them too.

Marsh's Law and Clive gave me a really fun moment with Mick Easterby, another trainer I've always had time for because he also knows and cares about horses.

Mick came up to me and said, "You're wasting your time today, son." I was wick with my answer and said, "I'm having a good day, Dad." It was all good banter, but I know that Mick knew Marsh's Law had been a good horse.

Marsh's Law was rated 57 and Mick's horse in the same race Scotton Banks was rated 168. It was no contest, if you just read figures.

If you then saw the start of the race you would have immediately said Mick had been right to say what he'd said. David Easterby was riding Scotton Banks and bloody hell did they go. Marsh's Law was at the back. Scotton Banks had won the King George VI Chase at Kempton and had very rarely been out of the placings throughout his career.

Marsh's Law was at the back. Ticking away. But by the time they turned for home he was in the front.

I couldn't believe my eyes. I thought there was no way this could be possible, but Clive was playing a blinder and had got Marsh's Law absolutely right. These two grand old horses were battling it out, but in the end it was a younger horse Concerto Collonges that won, Scotton Banks was second and Marsh's Law third. It really was a fabulous race.

Although Marsh's Law hadn't beaten Mick's horse, neither of us had won and when the horses came in I said, quite cheekily, but all in good sport, "You're wasting your time today, Dad."

Marsh's Law had a few more point-to-point races, including one where he looked really good again at Easingwold until he slipped on the turn and lost his footing.

Owning Marsh's Law was more than just a good experience for me. He was an honest, genuine horse and I owed him such a lot for the time he brought me back to fitness and back to life – and I wish to this day that I hadn't done what I ended up doing with him. He was a proper saint.

CHAPTER 14

Dotty Daydreamer

One of the biggest regrets in my life was selling Marsh's Law, but I just didn't have the stable space. I was trying to run racehorses and he'd run his race by now. I didn't have the pleasure of having room for horses that weren't going to run, or weren't bringing an income through coming here to be broken in. I had to make a living from what I was doing and so I made the choice to let him have a new home.

But that backfired on me big time because the woman who I sold him to tried to sue me for selling something that was unfit for purpose, and I know the horse suffered through the process. Unfit for purpose? She'd said she was going to use him for hacking? He was fine for that, or at least he was when he'd left me.

It is one of those things that sometimes happens in the horse world. There are people out there who will buy former racehorses but will have worked out a plan before they purchase that they can go back and actually sue people if things don't work out with the horse. She never told me, but her line of not fit for purpose was because she had ideas of running him. Really? She didn't even know how to look after him.

I am certain that there are some unscrupulous people out there who see trainers and owners as easy game. One of the problems some of them have is that they think that everyone who owns or trains racehorses is loaded and that if they are not happy with the horse they can simply cause trouble and worry the owner or trainer into paying out.

This new owner clearly hadn't done her homework very well, had she? She had seen me as a trainer and owner and thought she would get money out of me when he started going wrong on her.

This misguided woman, I can't bring myself to call her a lady, picked on the millionaire that was Cooper Wilson!

Oh, deary me, how wrong could one woman be? We'll call her Dotty Daydream, because that's what she was on both counts.

I stood my ground and won the court case.

Dotty had allegedly taken on Marsh's Law for hacking, but the reason why she had tried to take me for all of the three shillings and sixpence I had was that she had seen that he had won races and thought he could still do that. She bought the horse, in my opinion, to have this comeback. Get some cash.

When I sold him to Dotty I'd told her that he had suffered from colic a lot. What I'd worked out was that the problem was the hay. So, I never fed him hay. I'd go to roadside and I'd cut grass. I'd fill two bags a day, give him that and he never had colic. It was how you fed him and how you worked him to get him all balanced. From what I saw she didn't take any notice.

I had to take her back to court to get my expenses. I won that case as well, but I never got my expenses. She said she couldn't pay and then I found out that everything she had done in taking me to court had been on Legal Aid.

Dotty, oh deary me.

But there is a serious side to all of this, and I truly hope that my colleagues in the racing world today are not suffering right now from anyone like this.

CHAPTER 15

Racehorses in the 2000s

Life and racehorses shouldn't be about success or failure. There is only ever success if you are achieving something with an animal. I believe that a racehorse doesn't have to win races to be a success, it just has to perform to the best of its ability and if that ability isn't good enough to win a race then so be it.

That's not the horse's or the trainer's fault. It's not failure. It's always about experience and learning. And failure is such a very negative word and affects your state of mind. If you get up thinking you will fail, you will have failed before you've got out of bed.

I treasure what I have here at Manor Farm, today, in the countryside, with my horses, my family. I have the perfect life. I don't have lots of money. I'm not worth taking to the cleaners by any Dotty Daydreamers out there, but I do have purpose, I do have confidence, sometimes shaken every now and again like everybody else, but I have been successful in life in my own modest way.

I have all of these things today, because I've made it that way, because of all the things that have led to where I'm at now, and while some might look at this next roll of honour of racehorses I had between 2001 and 2008 and say, "Well, if you're supposed to be that good with horses, Cooper, what happened?" I can honestly tell you they were some of the happiest times of my life and I wouldn't be as in demand as I am today without the learning during those times.

Ideal Collonges was five years old when he first ran for me at Huntington in September 2001 with very popular jockey Russ Garrity. I'd bought him from Philip Hobbs, a trainer down in Devon, for £1,700 at the Doncaster sales. I'd been desperate for a new racehorse. He was a quirky horse, very highly strung and took a lot of settling before the race, so much so that you got the feeling he'd already run it before he started. Russ pulled him up. In his next race at Kelso he was so wound up that when the tapes went up he spun around and the jockey fell off. It was a lad called Alexander. Off the horse before the horse had started running! Oh my!

Bless him, the lad got back on but by the time he was back sorted Ideal Collonges was anything but ideal. He was four lengths behind. He jumped him off and then ran him off, pulling him up.

But at Sedgefield he ran alright. Alexander took him round nicely and he came in fourth. I felt we might have been getting somewhere, but after another disappointment, back at Sedgefield, I decided enough was enough. Ideal Collonges just wasn't cooperative. He didn't want to be a racehorse, and I sold him to a woman in Scarborough.

Amsara ran more races for me than any. She was a lovely, very honest mare who gave me great joy, but she was also the unluckiest horse. David Chapman let me have her for £300.

The only race we thought she could have won was when she ran at Cartmel where she finished fifth out of 14 in August 2002.

I said to the jockey JA Richardson, who rode her in most of her races, to front run her, but he never went. I'd wanted him to front run because I knew that her trouble was that she was a bit one-paced. She couldn't quicken. Her problem that day was she couldn't get to the front, but she did the very best she could and you couldn't argue with that.

But there was a race, her last as it proved to be, at Sedgefield where she really did look as though she had everything right. Lee Vickers was her jockey that day and he rode her beautifully.

I'd said to Lee to jump her off and get her away eight to nine lengths in front, let her tickle up the hill, let her get her second wind and go again. He did that and at the top of the hill Amsara was eight to nine lengths in front.

My sister Charlotte was so excited. We all were. "You're gonna win it," she said. I knew better to assume anything and said she had to jump the hurdles first. She was coming up to the last hurdle in the race – two furlongs out – and she broke down and pulled up well in front. Such a sad day. She had snapped her suspensory.

And if that wasn't bad luck enough, she then went and lost twin foals. Her leg injury then proved too bad, meaning she wasn't fit to ride, she lost so much weight and had to be put to sleep.

For a horse that was in low-grade races, she was really good. I put her to sleep myself and a few weeks later I was sitting in the kitchen at two in the morning and it was like she was there in front of me.

Amsara was still with me, her spirit, and for a while after that it was this lovely horse that was pushing me forward, and I needed that at that moment because I was starting to lose a little faith. That's how horses and their spirits can help too.

Horses and me, I know I keep writing it and saying it, but that's how it is and that's how everything has developed to the way things are today.

Next up was a true gentleman of a horse.

North was another horse from David Chapman. He let me have him, so that tells you something about his prospects if a respected trainer lets one go, doesn't it! North was too nice to be a racehorse. David knew, but he also knew that I'd give him a fair go and I did. North was actually quite a clever horse. It was as though he knew to only ever do just enough to keep everyone happy. He showed me that horses really do know what's going on. After five races I sold him to a girl in Newcastle and he did a wonderful job for her for about 12 years, just hacking about.

He'd been pulled up in four of his five races, but I was never dispirited by when we had to pull horses up. You see, I was working with horses that were never going to be world beaters, or even Easingwold beaters come to that. They were mostly either at the ends of their careers or ones that nobody else had wanted for obvious reasons, but they were what I could afford, and make no mistake a horse still needs to be fed whether it is one that wins hundreds of thousands of pounds' worth of prize money or it wins nothing at all.

I never blamed the horse. I always believed if the horse came back having had a good experience it would try harder next time. Sometimes it worked. Horses don't just live in the moment; they also have memories. Why do you think some horses are difficult? Often it is because of what they remember about their past.

And my view was that if they remembered having a good run, regardless of whether they went past the finishing post, that might help them in the future. I think that's where North was a canny lad. I think after the first few times he had been pulled up that he thought that would be good enough for him every time. But he was still a gentleman, even if he may have also been a bit cute.

I then had a series of horses that only ran once for me – Conundrum, Alizarin and Young Monash. They were all Irish-bred horses and I have to say, here and now, let's play this little lot for laughs right here because all three were a disaster!

I cannot remember being more embarrassed on a track than at Market Rasen in August 2003 and then at Hexham the following month.

Sit yourself down. Grab yourself a brew, but be careful how you drink it because there are certain parts that might make you splutter in hilarity – and I don't want you splashing this book, it's cost a lot to get it together, you know!

Are you sitting comfortably? Here we go.

It all started so innocently. Conundrum was loaded into the horsebox back home ready for his first race, at the lovely Market Rasen course in Lincolnshire. It was a lovely summer's day. The going was good to firm. His jockey was Christopher Murray, a well-respected jockey too.

My instructions to Christopher were to keep him on the inside. Christopher set off well with him. Conundrum was on the inside and going towards the first hurdle on the back straight. He was looking handy.

Then it happened.

He ran out, the blighter! Conundrum (what an apt name given what was happening) never jumped the hurdle. He got himself from the rail, around the hurdle and was recorded an 'R.O.'– run out! He ran out of the course! I decided immediately that he obviously did not enjoy it and never ran him again.

Christopher Murray won his next race that day on a horse called Sovereign.

Hold on to your mugs because that was just the taster for you, for what happened two weeks later.

My sister Charlotte owned Alizarin and I didn't want to run him. But Charlotte told me I couldn't just run him at home. By heck, what a quirky horse he was. I'd told Charlotte that he just was not the job. Whatever you did. He wasn't happy. Anyway, I gave in to her to keep the peace. It was a Sunday meeting too. I could feel it would be a waste of my Sunday, but hey-ho.

I rang Irish jockey Mickey Naughton, told him Alizarin was running and to do what he could with him. I had no prospect of success, even in the slightest, and I'm a positive person.

Off we went up to Hexham. It really is a lovely course and it was a warm, sunny September day. Barbara came too. At least we could have a family day out if nothing else. I was quite relaxed. You get that way when there's no expectation. I quipped To Mickey about which would come first, second and third and then my positive nature got the better of me, against my better judgement, and said maybe fourth of fifth would be a result? There were only seven in the race.

Alizarin was 66–1. I wouldn't have been surprised if it had been 2000–1. I said to Mickey that the horse was probably going to burn itself out before it got to the top of the hill and that if it wouldn't jump, not to force it.

Charlotte was excited. It was her horse after all. She was an owner. Barbara was up on the hill having a picnic up above the car and trailer. All was well with the world. Then the race started.

The horses appeared from having come up the hill. I saw them go by. One, two, three, just as I'd predicted, all up there and challenging. Four, five, six and … oh my Lord!

I looked down the course. I had to put the bins on he was that far off. Now, I'm not sure whether he was 75 lengths down off the nearest horse or 100 but it didn't matter. And I know

I've said this was all good experience for me, but let's strike that right here. This one most certainly wasn't. Honestly, that day I just wanted to hide. It was total embarrassment.

I shouted, "For goodness' (not the word I used, it has to be said) sake, Mickey! Pull it up!"

Mickey scrambled Alizarin over this hurdle and pulled it up within two yards of landing; and I said, "Put the flipping (not the word I used, it has to be said) thing in the trailer." I'll see you later. And that, as they say, was that.

The one horse I had that I cannot remember anything about is Young Monash. All I can tell you is that I'd taken him on from owner John Price and trainer Brian Rothwell. He ran once for me with jockey Lee Vickers and was pulled up at Sedgefield.

The most money I ever spent on a horse was one called Dark Knight. I knew he was a good horse. He cost £5,000. We pointed him in his first season and he showed a lot of promise, but fell three fences out at Easingwold as he was going to take the race on. Unfortunately, it had been a bad fall and he didn't run anymore that year.

I got him back fit and he was coming on nicely. I was confident he would do well and since I was really busy by this time with my RSPCA work, which we'll talk about soon, I put him with an excellent trainer Tim Walford at Sheriff Hutton.

Dark Knight had only been with Tim for five days when he ran at Bedale point-to-point and won by 30 lengths with Tim's son Mark as jockey. My first winner!

He ran again the following week at Easingwold, but was declared with blinkers on! I was told he needed them. It was a strange decision. He'd won by 30 lengths the previous week. It wasn't my decision, and I knew the horse. I knew that he would sulk and he did.

Arguably the most consistent horse I ever had was French-bred mare Sylvie D'Orthe that I bought from Martin Pipe at Doncaster. He was the highest-profile trainer I'd ever bought a horse from and I bought two from him the same day. Sylvie D'Orthe I bought as a four-year-old for £1,700; Gold For Me was a bay gelding that I bought for £2,000.

After having run a lot of yaks I'd moved up a step with Dark Knight and Sylvie D'Orthe. It just shows what a difference a little more money makes, in the case of Dark Knight, and buying from major trainers, in the case of Sylvie D'Orthe.

Sylvie D'Orthe ran six races for me. She was fourth out of six at Sedgefield; fifth out of nine at Sedgefield; sixth out of 12 at Kelso; fifth out of ten at Perth; seventh out of 17 at Huntington; and seventh out of 15 at Cartmel. Respectable finishes. And now I had horses that were finishing the races. I was moving up, just at the time I was getting busier with my RSPCA work. Bills needed to be paid.

If I'd had the money and I could have bought really good horses I now knew that I could have been a successful, winning racehorse trainer. It was Dark Knight and Sylvie D'Orthe that told me I could actually do this.

No matter what you do as a trainer, training horses is all about having the right horses and if you are an owner it is all about giving good money. Mine were all in the 0–90 ratings. It would have been nice to have had something in the 150s or bigger, but as I keep saying, I still loved the craic, the fact that I was a trainer, that I was an owner and that I was part of our wonderful world of horse racing – well, perhaps with the exception of Alizarin!

Sylvie D'Orthe was a horse with a big heart and when we went to Perth I went up there because the knowledge was that she was capable of winning it and on paper she should have been the winner.

Declan McGann rode a cracking race on her. Coming to the last fence he dropped his hands like he was going to pop the hurdle and win it. But as Declan dropped his hands going into the hurdle she nearly fell and lost all ground. She was a game horse though and got back her momentum. When she got to the finish we were just out of the placings.

We ran her at Sedgefield, where she finished fourth out of six in November 2005.

I said to Declan that when they had done one circuit to just squeeze her out and go for it. One of the horses was a natural front runner and I said that if he headed that, it would chuck the towel in and he'd go on and win. When they passed the winning post to go out for the last circuit they never moved up. When he came back in with Sylvie I asked why he hadn't gone where I'd told him?

Get ready for another learning curve here. This is straight out of a Dick Francis book.

Declan told me that Tony had told him not to. That was Tony Dobbin. Tony was in second, sat alongside him. When Declan was supposed to go Tony had told him not to go too early.

I couldn't believe what I was hearing. "Tony's told you not to go? Where did he flippin' (not the word I used, it has to be said) finish?" He had finished second. Tony had stitched Declan up. And me! That's why Declan didn't ride the horse at Carlisle next time out.

A young jockey called Cummings rode a cracking race on her at Carlisle, but she struggled going up the hill and wasn't blessed with a speedy finish, but she had a big heart. I finally had a horse that may not have been the best by any means but gave me all she had and some fun times. She finished every race, never finished better than fourth and never worse than seventh and often in decent fields. I sold Sylvie to a good friend as a hack.

Gold For Me was nowhere near as successful, but success is all relative and he at least finished both his races at Huntington and Towcester. The great AP McCoy had even fancied Gold For Me when the horse had run at Towcester. Tony told Declan McGann, who was riding Gold For Me, that if the horse was ridden right it could win.

He'd said that he knew the horse and knew it was good enough and to sit him in and three fences out to pull him out and set him on to the front. When Declan told me, I remember saying, "Well we've got to listen to the man that knows, happy days." Gold For Me finished last of nine runners – and worse still down the back straight I'd seen him go 'bleurgh' and I had known there and then that he wouldn't be coming home with us.

Sylvie D'Orthe and Dark Knight had given me hope. They had proved to me I was worthy of a trainer's licence, but to be fair I really believe the work I had done with all of the horses that I'd been running had been worthwhile.

After Sylvie D'Orthe my work with the RSPCA was taking over my life and I really didn't have the time to give properly to training racehorses. I knew from David Chapman and all of my time with racehorses that attention to detail is paramount. You can only get the best out of a horse if you give that commitment and in the last two years of holding my trainer's permit I really couldn't give the attention to detail any longer.

The Jolly Trolley, All For Jake, Saxon Mist, Mary Buck and River Trapper were my final fling between 2006 and 2009. Only River Trapper of the five started twice; and only one of them wasn't pulled up, The Jolly Trolley.

Jockey Dougie Costello brought The Jolly Trolley home sixth from eight at Uttoxeter. Irish Jockey Joe Draper pulled up All For Jake at Cartmel. The horse was 11 years old and he had a bit of a leg problem and was half-hearted in his running. He was another of those who I was running to keep the peace. People were saying 'to get him run' and in those days I was letting people influence me.

I could see it was the wrong thing. I said to Joe to just enjoy the ride and pull up All For Jake if he had to. That's what he did.

I'd bought him thinking he was going to be alright, but back home in training he wasn't as good as I thought and I didn't like running horses just for the sake of running them.

I sold him to a woman over in Manchester who then sold him to a woman called Ruby Walsh in West Sussex. Up to about two years ago (and I am writing this in July 2022) the horse was still alive. That would have made him 25 years old, so again another horse I had that has lived a long and happy life.

I never had any faith in Saxon Mist. I bought him out of Doncaster for about £2,000. He didn't show any form at all back home. I was paying attention to detail as much as I could, but he was proving very hard work, but again I was being pressed to run him.

So, I took him to Stratford on a Sunday and jockey Keith Mercer came back in after pulling him up and I asked what had been wrong. Keith said exactly the same as I'd already thought, "Your horse has no faith in himself." I sold him to a girl in Scarborough.

Mary Buck. Oh My! She has to be one of the few horses to have been declared for two races, get to the start in two races and only run in one! In her first race she was meant to run at Stratford at the same meeting as Saxon Mist. She didn't even set off!

She pulled up before going across the start, which meant to add insult to injury that she wasn't even recorded as running! Because she didn't. She buried the jockey at the start.

She very clearly did not want to run because at Catterick a month later in a bumper race, on the flat, she came round the turn and must have looked at where she had come out, because she stopped. At least it was an easy walk back for her and the jockey CJ Callow.

Which brings us to the last horse I ever had as a trainer, River Trapper. He might only have had two runs for me in National Hunt, but ran 11 altogether with nine in point-to-point where his best place was third at Easingwold.

River Trapper had been with Henrietta Knight before coming to me. Four years before coming to me he'd won at Newbury in 2004, but that had been a long time ago in this horse's career. My sister Edna owned him. He was pulled up at Catterick and Sedgefield by jockey Sesston, but we had some fun with him in point-to-point, especially when Laura Eddery was on him and he started to run well. He was one gear short of really challenging for a win.

He was a very careful horse, another gentleman and he gave us some really nice moments.

Although I have worked with people's horses at home, I've never gone back into being a racehorse trainer since 2009. I don't have my permit now. In some ways I wish I still had it.

If I could attract sponsors in order to do the job right, then maybe I would go back. I certainly loved being a trainer, but money was always too tight to be able to invest in the right horses, and you do burn yourself out, especially when you need to have other incomes to pay for it all – and you need resilience, you need to keep positive when you get deflated, you need faith.

But what I got out of it was experience you could never have got out of a book. I learned how to make decisions and how not to be influenced by others. I know one thing for sure. You can't sit at home and wait for it to happen. My advice to anyone is if you want to do something do it with all your heart and soul and you will always find there is satisfaction in that.

You've got to have the heart. When Amsara had gone and yet kept pushing me forward through her spirit, she gave me the faith to never give up. She gave me that confidence in life.

Sylvie D'Orthe and Dark Knight brought my dream back to life, they rekindled the flame when it may have been on the wane. I'd had dreams, like anyone else when they are trying to achieve something.

Your dreams are there to encourage you to go and do what you feel you need to do. And if you do, if you go for those dreams, you never fail. Okay, there are plenty of times when you don't feel as though you are getting there, but you need to remain positive. Sometimes that is difficult, sometimes really hard, because of what you are having to cope with elsewhere, but even when your positivity does occasionally wane you just need to remember your dreams and look at how far you've come.

Being a racehorse trainer, even just a permit holder as I was, able to run my own horses in bumpers, National Hunt and point-to-point was an amazing life experience, but not just that, it was also a deeply spiritual experience. I learned so much about myself, about my horses and I really did, as people say, live the dream.

CHAPTER 16

The Horse Ambulance & the RSPCA

There are moments in your life when everything seems to just click. It's a bit like when you find out what makes a horse click, and that's how it was for me in my life at around the same time as I was having my most successful days as a trainer with Dark Knight and Sylvie D'Orthe.

I'd had some pretty dark times with the bus company since my stroke and without going into too much detail about it all here, because Country Travel was only ever a means to an end, an income generator, the bus company folded and went bust in 2004.

The killer had been that I'd had health issues in 2003 which led to me not being able to drive for a while again.

Now, in order to keep positive here, let's just say that I blame myself for the way things had gone with the bus business since my stroke and then again with the relapse when I couldn't be hands-on or look after it properly. I think that will cover it.

My friends know very differently and know what really happened, but while that was a part of my life it's not what you want to read about here. It's not why I'm writing this book. Let's stay positive, because that's the best way to be.

So, in October 2004 the bus company part of my life was over when it went into administration and I was declared bankrupt.

That'll do for Country Travel. What had started as running a minibus for young farmers' clubs and pub sports teams had served me well, but it had also taken its toll on my health.

Now, it was a new time.

Ironic, isn't it, that the next year was to be so good. Great with racehorses and my training – and a brand-new venture that led me even further down the road to where I am today.

Me and horses, all the way, from now on.

I bought a horse ambulance.

It was pure luck that I got into what happened next, or was it the spirit world?

This ambulance had been advertised by JSW in Northallerton in 2005. The JSW people are fantastic at making bespoke horseboxes, probably one of the best in the business, and they had manufactured this from a readymade trailer. We added a winch and a sling for transportation purposes and horse comfort.

My idea had been to run a horse ambulance service that would take horses to vets for them to decide what was best to do with them. My timing of purchase was spot on because just at that time the police at Thirsk were wanting a horse transporter for a Shetland pony that was injured.

I took the pony back to Fawdington Lodge. Then the RSPCA got involved as they needed transportation of horses to their centre in County Durham. I was your man.

But then they couldn't cope with the volume of horses up there.

That's how this new business grew – and how!

In the coming years I would have more than 500 horses at any one time here, there and everywhere at nine locations and with a team of 12 people.

Not long after I'd started with the horse ambulance, and with the work with the RSPCA taking off, we moved to Witherholme Hall at Whenby. It sounds very grand, doesn't it? But it wasn't a hall at all, more like a big farm cottage.

Fawdington Lodge was having some work done to it at the time. The owners had said that we had to move out while it was sorted, and I'd met Fred Niceguy (I've changed his name here for a good reason) who owned Witherholme Hall and who'd said that so long as we paid the rent we could be there as long as we liked.

We needed more space as a family because Barbara and I now had three kids – Alex, Eleanor, and Katy who had just been born in 2006.

I'd told Helperby Estates that we wouldn't be moving back to Fawdington Lodge once the renovation work had been completed because of our new agreement with Fred.

Sadly, just two years later, Fred passed away and let's just say things didn't work out with those who had inherited, and so we were on our way again around 2008 and this time to the village where we are today in Oulston.

I had rung Steve Wombwell at Newburgh Estates about any possible properties that were available to rent. I'd driven his and his father Lord Wombwell's children to school when I had the buses. I explained what had happened and Steve said that they were just in the middle of renovating Hope Cottage in the village, but that we could have that. We had it three years before moving to Manor Farm on the edge of the village where we have now been since 2012.

And the purpose of telling you all of that is because when the RSPCA work started to grow I was able to keep horses at Witherholme as we had a big shed that I had converted to stables. The RSPCA didn't have enough room to stable the number of horses that they were receiving calls about.

I said I had plenty of room at Witherholme and I was soon up to ten horses that I was looking after, but when Fred passed away in 2007 I began renting Lund Farm at Easingwold which had 29 acres and accommodation for 40 horses and in the coming years the RSPCA business went totally bananas. It didn't matter where I rented or how much accommodation I had, we just kept filling it all up. It amazed me just how many horses were being mistreated and were going through the RSPCA.

I built up a team, starting at Witherholme, and the first member of the team was a girl called Sarah Johnson.

Sarah was a wonderful girl and I couldn't have done it without her. Next was another fabulous girl called Carol Cornforth. When Sarah left to become a nurse, Carol became yard manager and she really was right for the job. She cared just as much as me about the horses. Debbie Howe joined the team and was also very good and then Sarah came back on board. They were all then based at Lund Farm. It was a team I could trust, every one of them, and that allowed me to go off to a job, hitch up, drive off and leave them to it.

Sarah became the nurse she wanted to be, and she saw that every horse got their medication. She kept all of the records. We then got a young girl called Becky Mills who used to drive from Whitby every day. She was fantastic too, really committed. Then we had Sarah Perry. My word, could she break a horse in! And so could Carol. She was one heck of a horsewoman.

These girls, and others, helped me so much and I will be forever grateful for their time, commitment, support and most of all the love of horses that they showed every single day.

You see, we all tend to think of that saying 'A puppy is not just for Christmas' when people buy them for loved ones, but later find they can't look after them. Maybe it is the same with ponies or horses, it certainly seemed to be.

I would never say no to the RSPCA about taking on any horse

because I care passionately about horses and their welfare, plus this was my new income. I was paid for picking up, transporting, feeding and stabling.

One of the problems the RSPCA have, and it's not their fault, is how long the legal side takes. And it often takes an interminably long time. This is where our legal system does not help horses.

In the UK there has to be legal proof that horses have either been mistreated, mishandled, been malnourished or abused in any way and courts will allow the accused to adjourn the court hearing because they 'need more time to consider' and are not ready for judgement. It all delays the sometimes inevitable for horses that are not well and leads to them being put to sleep when sometimes they could have been saved.

Over in New Zealand the RSPCA often have it all settled in court the next morning.

This backlog that is created through our legal system was part of the reason why I had to keep taking on even more premises and became a kind of boarding centre for horses and ponies to be rehomed by the RSPCA from 2009 to 2013.

I took on 54 boxes and 100 acres in Raskelf and then I took on another farm in the same village, then another just outside Easingwold that could take on 300 horses. The girls were working across all of it. The girls and I had it running like clockwork and there wasn't a horse on the place that I didn't know where it had come from or its history. We had 517 horses on at one time and all from starting with stabling one Shetland pony!

Once we had reached quite a number of horses I had Mike Hogg the regional manager of the RSPCA come to see me. What me and the girls were doing was now a substantial part of the RSPCA's work with horses in the north of England and we were also getting horses sent from other parts of the country.

Mike wanted to know more about what was going on here and also, presumably, where all this money for stabling and looking after the horses was going.

He was a good man and we worked well together. We both had lots of ideas of how we could help the horses. That's what I cared about most. Mike liked what we were doing and had a lot of faith in me.

I'd worked out through our own experience with how long we had each horse here that by the time court hearings had finished it meant that we would have a horse for an average of about 18 months.

And we worked hard with each one. We worked on getting the horses properly fed, back fit and mentally sound where possible, because tragically, in many cases they weren't and ever so many had to be put to sleep.

These horses had been badly let down by their owners and while myself and the girls tried our level best, and in my opinion worked some miracles, we were not miracle workers.

Many of these horses had suffered and for many there really was nothing that could be done to bring them back because of neglect or harm. In hundreds of cases the best we could do was give a good life for what remained for them.

But there are important facts of life about horses and anyone taking ownership of one from the RSPCA.

They will generally only be taken on by people if they can ride them or work them in some way – and hundreds of them were now not up to that – and there aren't enough charity horse places around that can afford to keep the number of horses that come through the RSPCA every year. That's why so many have to be put to sleep. It's not nice, but in the cases I have seen it has also been a blessed relief for the horse.

Where we, the girls and I, offered something different was in using our skills to bring those that could be saved back to a normal life. During the 18 months we had them we would begin their rehabilitation. We would break them in if they had never had that done before. We had horses that hadn't been touched for years due to their owners' neglect and we did all we could to bring them back around so that they could go to new owners.

Some at the RSPCA Felledge Animal & Rescue Centre in Chester-le-Street would tell me that the work we were putting into the horses would be wasted if they, the RSPCA, lost the court case and the horses had to go back to their owners.

My argument was that it didn't matter because if they went back they would be going back as better ponies or horses and if the owner then had any sense they would sell quickly, so we were giving back a better horse and God willing the horse would end up in the right place where it was appreciated and looked after correctly.

When it turned out the RSPCA couldn't rehome horses quickly enough, Mike (Hogg) gave me free rein on rehoming them myself and I ended up rehoming 180 horses a year for a three-year period. Previously the RSPCA at Felledge had been rehoming significantly less.

This is how good we were at looking after horses and bringing them back to life and to new owners.

We had one horse that I'd been involved in rehoming that became UK Horse Endurance Champion a couple of years later. That was a real result, especially as the girls at RSPCA Felledge had told me to shoot it.

And that wasn't the only time I'd been told that. I was told that if I hadn't shot a little grey horse by Monday that this girl from Felledge would get somebody down to shoot it.

By then I knew what was really happening and it was nothing to do with horses. It was petty politics.

Why is it that people play silly games? And especially why play them when they are affecting animals' lives and wellbeing? I had thought that the RSPCA would be full of people with only the animals' wellbeing at heart. How wrong was I?

I assumed the girls at Felledge saw me as a threat. I was looking after more horses than them and now I was rehoming more than them, so it appeared they wanted to keep telling me who was in control. Well, I've got to tell you, it wasn't them!

I have the greatest respect for the RSPCA as an institution. Their work with all animals has been phenomenal over so many years and they have absolutely fabulous people working within the organisation, I also had a great respect for Mike Hogg, but the two girls I was having to talk with? Nah.

I rehomed hundreds of RSPCA horses. I gifted them rather than selling them because if you've sold more than a certain number of horses in a year you can be classed as a dealer and that was never my reason for finding them good homes. It was all about me and horses.

I lost the contract with the RSPCA. To my mind it was all because of the petty politics being played by these two unmentionables. They just tried to make my life hell. It was a shame. And it was a shame for my team too. If only these people had known the real impact they'd had on a dozen others who were all working so hard.

I miss having all those horses around and I miss having the team we had, but by then the Yorkshire Horseman was set to start riding high!

CHAPTER 17

David & Marion Chapman

Tuning into horses and telling people about their horses now comes naturally and spiritually to me. I don't have to force it.

Trainer David Chapman had nothing to do with that, but it was David who gave me that confidence to believe in myself. He was very similar to me in some ways, which is why I was able to talk with him.

David died quite suddenly in 2011. I'd been talking to him about a grey horse just a few days earlier and I had said he should send it to me, that I would sort it out for him.

Marion, David's wife, told me afterwards that just before he had passed away David had said, "Let Cooper have that grey horse." I was blown away. It was typical of David to be thinking about his horses right up until the end, but I was really touched that he should mention me too. I knew they both respected me, Marion and David.

If ever my faith in people had been properly restored after some horrendous schooldays and being looked down on as a jug-eared youth, not being worthy of being spoken to by the gentry, it had been through this lovely couple.

I thanked Marion who, as you remember, I always called 'madam'.

Marion said, "David wanted you to have the horse, Cooper, but I don't want you to have it because it is very dangerous and

I really would be worried if you took it."

I knew what she meant. I'd had the horse with me by that time and it really was a nutter and also wasn't that special. Marion had known this too, and she wanted to do right by me. She knew I'd be daft enough to try with it. I'd give anything a chance.

I said, "I tell you what, madam, if it pleases you. What I mean is that you didn't need to make this call, you should do what you feel is right for the horse."

Then Marion showed me just how much she thought of me and said, "But I've got something else here."

Marion gave me a chestnut broodmare's foal. If ever I'd had the wind taken out of my sails by the generosity shown to me by anyone it was in this moment. David had given me a lot of horses over the years but this one from Marion, well what a gift!

The foal was ten days old and Marion gave me him instead – and with the chestnut mare!

What I would have loved to have done with him would have been to train him myself but just as he was about to go into training I lost the RSPCA contract and I was rebuilding my other work again and needed every penny.

I put the horse into training with Rebecca Menzies at Howe Hills in Sedgefield and then sold him to a syndicate because I couldn't afford him on my own. This horse had a great career. He was rated as high as 123, he won at Wetherby and Cartmel and finished in the first three 18 times. He was some horse.

He's called Captain Mowbray. I named him after Mowbray House where David used to train and so far as I'm concerned David was the captain.

Rebecca absolutely idolised the horse, the syndicate did too. He gave them all such good times and I had a spiritual connection with Captain Mowbray all the time.

In his last race, Hexham, 2 September 2020, he broke down. I knew he'd had a dodgy front leg and he was given time out from racing. He'd come back in July that year where he'd come third at Cartmel.

At Hexham he looked really good. He was five lengths in front and seemingly going on to win his race until he jumped the last and broke down, which saw him finish fifth because of his leg.

His racing career had started at Kelso in November 2015 when he'd finished third. The news after the race at Hexham in September 2020 was that he would have to go to Liverpool to have stem cell treatment as he'd blown his suspensory ligament and then he would need eight months box rest before he could go back into training.

He'd just had a year and a half out before these past two races. It was going to cost the syndicate £20,000. It was going to be a lot of money for them to find. It would have been a lot of money for anybody to find.

Understandably they had put their money in to see their racehorse run. There was another option, but to be fair to the syndicate they didn't like the option of having him put to sleep, he'd meant more to them than that.

Rebecca wanted my opinion.

I was in no doubt. This horse still means the world to me. He's my physical as well as spiritual connection with David.

I said, "Bandage him up, put him on the wagon, take him back to the yard and I'll pick him up in a week."

Captain Mowbray came back to me and I had him back sound in the saddle and in work within eight weeks compared to the eight months they'd anticipated. What got him back was me and him working together.

I took his bandages off. In the eyes of the veterinary and

equine world it may have looked as though I was taking a gamble, but in my eyes I was doing what was right for that injury and for Captain Mowbray.

I wanted him to realise he had a bad leg, that's why I took them off. I put him out in the field, rather than in a box, because I wanted him to feel it so that he would compensate for it and in so doing allow it to heal naturally.

I would put my hands on him and did the universal energy thing through reiki to slow his mind and body down so that he could carry this injury without making it any worse.

As time went on this tendon stretched and then became tighter and as the tendon becomes tighter it knits back together. At that point I was able to bring Captain Mowbray into controlled work, which then made the leg bind better.

Captain Mowbray is 11 years old now, not a bad age for a jumper. Red Rum won the Grand National at 12 years old. I know that he could jump again now but he's never run again since September 2020.

But he's now living as good a life as I can give him. He's back with me and he is here in memory of David and that is just fantastic.

And that's not the end of it either. Captain Mowbray went to his first RoR class recently and won in the show ring. He's back winning. I smile every morning I see him, thinking back to those days with David. His granddaughter Ruth Carr has taken over now and she's a good lass. It's a funny old world. If I'd known about David not losing out on money when I had the injury at his place, I would have stayed with him and he'd always said since that there was a job for me if I'd wanted it, but then I wouldn't have done all that I have since.

Captain Mowbray and me. That's really still David and me.

CHAPTER 18

Polo Horses

My international reputation for helping 'those that can't speak for themselves' began while we were at Witherholme Hall and it came about due to a story that appeared in local newspapers and was then picked up by the *Sunday Express* and then an international equine magazine. This was all in 2007.

Up until then I might have been in some kind of witness protection programme for all the wider horse world knew about me, but I went viral as 'The Man Who Listens To Horses' and whoomph! My phone never stopped ringing for weeks. In fact, it hasn't stopped since then.

The story included quotes from a woman who had been blown away by what I had done for her horse, and this chap called Sandy had read it, so he contacted me, and he sent a grey polo horse. That then saw me looking after Argentinean polo horses.

Sandy was an Englishman with a big estate in Argentina and in me he found someone he could trust. He was having trouble with the first grey horse and I took it and got it right. I gave it that attention to detail I talked about earlier that involves the power of thought, with and of the horse.

We all know there is no way on earth a horse can talk to you, as I've said before. But you can listen to a horse and you can tune into it. This grey had been rearing up and throwing himself backwards and had injured its back.

I told Sandy that the reason it had this behavioural problem wasn't down to the horse's fault. I knew through listening and the power of the horse's mind that he couldn't forgive those around him. That was what I'd picked up. That was why it was going wrong.

After picking that up it was then down to my bit as the Yorkshire Horseman to get him back right. I did the physio on him and even though I'm not a qualified physiotherapist I know how to do it. It was steady slow work, as backs are for humans as well as animals, and he needed to be able rebuild the damaged muscle. I did the manipulation and the reiki on him.

The reiki would relax the horse's mind and once the mind is relaxed so is the body and your blood circulation can flow easier because you've no tension.

Then the horse, because you're also feeding it good food, can absorb its nutrients correctly into the blood stream. It will then be able to carry oxygen and hydration that a muscle needs – a horse is oxygen and hydration, everything else is secondary.

After seeing what I had done with the grey and being amazed that I'd turned him around Sandy started sending over racehorses from Argentina that he wanted turning into polo ponies. He told me he was selling them to royalty.

My word! I'm no longer some oik in the countryside, I'm preparing horses for kings and queens! You could have pinched me at that point to check I wasn't dreaming. From string bridles to your majesty!

I was getting horses from South America, ten or a dozen at a time, acclimatising them, working with them and then off they went to Ascot or Midhurst in West Sussex, to the home of polo at Cowdray Polo Club.

And here's a beautiful footnote to the story about the polo horses. In January of this year (2022) I received a call from a woman who had reached that point where her horse needed to be put to sleep.

I do hear all of the sad tales, but I also know what people are going through. Nobody wants to say goodbye.

I said to her, "You don't have to make excuses to me my love, because I know people don't make this kind of decision unless it's forced upon them. I'll come."

When I arrived, this old pony came slowly up to me and I just had this glimpse that we'd met before.

Now, when I'm in that situation sometimes I'm not sure whether I'm just thinking it or getting it as a message, because the thought and message are very close. It's blurry as to which it is.

I looked at the pony and my thought was, "What a rough 'owd thing this is."

Then the woman said, "Poor Maraposa," and I said, "I beg your pardon, Maraposa?" I then said, "Polo pony?" She said, "Yes, it is, that's right."

"Well, blow me down," I said. "I had that horse 15 years ago." I said, "How old is she now, because she was already about 18 when I had her." She said, "34." I said, "That horse came to me from Argentina." I said, "It had a heart murmur, and the vet had said it would drop dead all those years ago, and here I am today." It was time for Maraposa to go, but what a life I had been able to give her.

CHAPTER 19

The Yorkshire Horseman Begins:
The Readings

My readings have always been something I've been able to give but in more recent years the demand for them has gone absolutely crazy. I now spend most of my time either on the road, on the phone or working with Alex and Esme on rehabilitating horses here at home.

And the way things have been going it is proving to be far more of the first two. Fortunately, we are a great team, myself, Alex and Esme, Alex's partner.

Word of mouth is an incredibly powerful thing and I have found that each time I give readings on the phone or by visiting, that word gets around pretty fast and more calls and visits go into the diary.

People are naturally inquisitive, some have belief, some are sceptical, but my view is that I am always there first and foremost for the horse. Of course, if that helps the owner too then so much the better, but I don't dress things up. I tell it like it is. If I feel something, if I'm being told something, it is my duty to pass that on to the owner, even when it is something they may not want to hear. I speak for each horse.

I'm not infallible. I don't always get it right, but nine times out of ten I do. I'm not doing this because I want to, but because I have to. I have been given a spiritual, intuitive gift that maybe not many others will ever have and that is what has led to my incredibly popular road trips that see me regularly visiting places like Northern Ireland and Orkney.

Everything I say is what I'm picking up intuitively. I can't tell you why I do, I just do. After I've given my readings it is sometimes only then that I will see the horse, and if it's a phone reading I definitely won't see it.

What is important for me to stress is that while all of this is the bit that gives me my name – the readings, what people call the heebie-jeebie stuff – it is only part of Cooper Wilson, the Yorkshire Horseman. It is the part that either you believe in or you don't. All I can say is that my record speaks for itself.

I don't know why I am clairsentient, clairvoyant, psychic, spiritualist or a medium. I just know that what I do helps horses and owners.

I can do readings for people too. I can tell people what's in their past, what is in their future and what is in their horse's past and future. I've been able to do it, like a gypsy, since I was a kid.

I've never researched. I'm what you call a self-taught medium. I can't read a book let alone write one, which is why I brought in Chris (Berry) to do this for me, but that also means I can't be influenced by what's in a book.

The stag was my education. It showed me that life here does come to an end, but that it is not ended when we have finished here, that it carries on to the other spiritual side. It's just about having faith in what you can't prove.

I'd started with some yard visits around 2005 and 2006. It had all come about through my work dealing with horses that were to be put to sleep.

I might go to a place where I was supposed to be assisting with a horse's demise, but then I might say, "Why are you doing this? This horse shouldn't be put down." And I would explain what I was getting back from the horse.

One reading that sticks out in my mind was from a woman who rang saying she had a black mare. I told her about it with hardly any more information than that, just a black mare.

Everything was good. I got near the end of the reading and then I said, "I've got a black and white one now. I mean that I can see a black and white one around you."

The woman wasn't angry, she was just trying to make sense of it all. Then she said, "Well I …" And she stopped, briefly before carrying on.

She said, "Oh, I had one 20 years ago." I said that's the one but it's telling me about a chestnut pony that's lame." She said, "Are you sure?" And I said, "Over the phone it's difficult for me to understand whether it's alive or dead, but you've got a pony close to you that's lame." She said, "That's my next-door neighbour's."

"Well," I said, "tell him not to have it put down."

She said, "That's what they're going to do." I said, "Tell them they've not to." And I told her what was wrong with it and to tell the man, if he wanted to, to ring me.

He rang me. He said, "Oh Jesus, I don't believe in this sort of thing, but what you've said to her I'm having to follow."

I said, "There's nothing to be frightened of, but your wishes are to be granted."

"Oh Jesus," he said. "This is strange." He said, "My biggest wish is for my horse to be sound for my kid to ride."

I said, "Your wish will be granted, but the only way you can achieve your wish, and the only man in Ireland that I know that can help you, is a long way up the road."

"By jove, me boy, it won't be a problem won't that." I said,

"Right, ring this feller and tell him to ring me. I'll tell him what to do."

This blacksmith rings me and says, "This feller rings me from the south, what do you want me to do?" So, I told him. "And believe you me," I said, "it will work."

The man from Southern Ireland travelled seven hours to the north to get this pony shod. He then took the pony back home and I told him that unfortunately he'd have to do that trip twice.

When he took the pony back the second time the pony was right. The first time had been to tidy it up and the next time was to finish the job. The pony went back and everything was fine.

I told him the pony might get a bit cheeky, but that's where his daughter would learn about the pony and how to ride it, but that he hadn't to be frightened to put her on it. I told him, "He's a quirky pony, but he's safe."

What was wrong with him? His feet were imbalanced, and the horse wasn't on the right diet.

The owner had done the right thing. He had contacted the vet, which you must always do. I am not a vet. I must stress this.

The owner had listened to the vet who had said that the pony wanted this and that. I knew that the horse couldn't heal while he was on the diet that he'd been given, that he had to have the right nutrients going into his system. It had been the vet that had said there was nothing the owner could do but put him down.

The owner went up to see Jamie Quinn, the blacksmith twice and the pony was successful.

And you'd think that might be a happy ending? Well, not straight away. The next thing I know the blacksmith in the south has been and shod the horse and he's lame!

What had happened was the owner's local vet had advised

him not to feed the horse! Honestly!

Well, you and I can't go to work on an empty belly and work all day and neither can a horse. No wonder he was lame! I rang Jamie and told him what had happened and we redeemed the situation – and had a happy horse, owner and daughter!

CHAPTER 20

The Road Trips:
Northern Ireland

I've had some amazing stories on my road trips. I really need to get a trip into Southern Ireland. I normally go for three days at a time and I've been back to Northern Ireland this year (2022) and during that time I gave readings for about 40 horses. It's pretty much non-stop from getting off the plane.

My first road trip was to Northern Ireland in 2011 and I now do road trips there and Orkney every year.

The road trip idea came about when I'd met Colleen Letters from Northern Ireland at the horse sales in York. I'd bought a pony for Alex that day. We had got friendly and she had set up a trip. I was keen to prove what I could do and on that first visit I blew everybody away – and from then on it just went whoosh!

Colleen is a wonderful woman who rehabilitates horses and knows what I can do. These days it is Colleen who will pick me up from Belfast Airport and she will say, "We're just going to stop off at this wee place on the way back," and we get the job done.

It will be around seven o'clock when I get off the plane, and I have learned that Colleen's arithmetic could do with a bit of sharpening up! Only one or two to do she says!

I'll get there, to this 'wee place' and there will be eight or nine or ten to do! I'm there till one o'clock or half past one in the morning. Then, and only then, do we get to Colleen and her partner Chris's place for some well-earned kip.

I'm then sent to bed with the words, "We need to be on the road at half eight in the mornin', so don't lie in!" The next day I'm at it here, there and everywhere until midnight. They are fantastic people and we have become great friends. You can't get better, and because I'm not having to drive that really helps.

We put something on social media the Friday before I'm going to go and you can guarantee I'm fully booked within a few hours. I very rarely see the same people twice because Colleen keeps a waiting list and those who have been just can't get back in that often.

I go over on the Monday, start readings on that evening and I'm there all day Tuesday and every bit of Wednesday that I can, before getting back to the airport at four o'clock. It's full-on and in that time I see 40–50 horses.

Sometimes they all converge in a yard where I can do a few (that's often Colleen's few rather than mine!) and then off we go, back on the road and do a few more. We tap away at this until one o'clock both evenings I'm there.

I've found that Irish people are very much on the fence until you've proved yourself and then it's like, "What the fettlin' hell?" They then become your friend – for life.

I'll never forget the first road trip I ever had.

Chris Connon, Colleen's partner, pulls up in this knackered old Isuzu Trooper, a right farmer's truck that you ever saw. I'm stood in the car park with a fag on.

My first thought wasn't from any celestial angels or spiritual guides. It was what the fettling hell have I come to! I get in his truck and I sit in the seat. I thought, that's wet.

Chris Connon says in his broad Irish accent, "You alright

there?" I said, "Seat's a bit damp." He says, "Oh, it's that fettling old diesel tank." He'd only had a diesel can on it and it had leaked! I'm sat in a pool of fettling diesel, fortunately I'd just put my fag out before getting in. I thought, to use an Irish term, "Holy Mother Mary and the wee donkey, I won't be striking a match in here otherwise I really would be lighting up!"

Chris is a proper grand feller, a real man. He said that first night, "I've to take you to so-and-so, there's a few there to do." We get to this first place. It was 11 in the morning when I'd landed that first time. I asked a question of them 12 hours later when we were still there having done 25 by then and I think Colleen must have got her degree in arithmetic from Chris. She'd been there when we'd arrived. I asked her how many more were to be done? She said, "Oh there's a few more." We didn't get out of there until two o'clock in the morning!

We were in this round building, there were stables all around and I'm in the middle and there's horses coming to me, being brought in on trailers, coming off the trailers.

I thought, I'll have a fag and as I looked up, I'm not kidding you, there's another ten trailers coming in at half past ten at night. All to the one spot, all waiting for a reading, queuing, loving it. Chris asked how I was doing.

I said, "I don't know how I'm going to get on with this next one. He's well and truly f***ed." I'm sorry everybody. I've resisted up until now and you can make up your own word there, but truly there was no other word for him. I added for good measure, "He's no good, absolutely knackered."

Chris said, "How do you get round that one?" I said, "You watch …"

I'd just finished with one that I'd said wasn't right and the woman was happy with what I'd said.

And the next one comes in, the one that's knackered.

The horse is stood behind me and this woman has got pink and blue hair, piercings and tattoos and she's like a matchstick.

I said, "I tell you what he wants," and she says, "What?" I said, "He wants a good feed. You feed him well and you'll get the best out of him. He's a little bit uncomfortable with what you're doing because he's hungry."

Pink and Blue said, "Ohhhh, he gets plenty of hay." I said, "It's not enough love, this horse is ambitious, he's got a dream, and he's only got the dream because he's had a taste of it." I said that I had no idea what he'd been successful at, but Chris told me later it had been a successful hunt horse.

I said, "You take him home. He knows what he's missing and he knows what he wants, but he can't get what he wants because he's not strong enough or fed well enough to get the strength, so the reason why you're getting difficulties is because he knows he's not strong enough to do what his true ability can give him."

I said, "You've got a real top-class, one-day eventer here and he'll go in the show ring and clean up. He's probably a HOYS horse or a Dublin horse. She said, "Oooh …" and suddenly everybody else was smiling.

I got to another one and it was quite a different story.

I said, "I'll tell you what love. I'm going to say three words: shoot the thing." I may have used four words thinking back. She said, "Really?" I said, "Yes, before it kills somebody because this is an outright bastard."

By this time it's late at night. I've done at least eleven hours here and I'm getting tired. You can get mentally as well as physically drained doing my job.

When that happens, any bits of sugar-coating that I sometimes use to soften a blow to an owner is gone. I'm not thinking about what I'm saying anymore, I'm just saying it. And she stood there.

For what I do you should never look at the facial expression because it can be so misread. You can think an expression means, 'He's bloody well got this wrong', but it can just as easily be, 'How the hell has he got that information?'

I look anywhere but at facial expressions. I look, if you will, as though I have my crystal ball at the floor. To me it's the hard way, but the honest way if I get it wrong.

I'd picked up on this horse's temper and dangerous side and I couldn't see how to get it out of that dangerous mindset. The first thing I got was 'get it shot'.

I said, "Now look, I'm not going to waste any more of your or my time on this because I can't see you achieving any more with it." I then said, "How far off the truth am I?"

She said, "I don't know how you did that." I said, "Are you brave enough to have him put down, to make everybody safe?"

She said, "Yes. It is very nasty and it is dangerous to go in with." I hadn't even looked at it, it was behind me. She was in front.

When I get it like that I have to believe what I'm getting and I have to be honest, give what I'm getting to the owner. It had proved a bit of a shock to hear it from me – and like I said it was that time of night when I was thinking I wanted to get things over and done with, to go and get my kip, but that would have been the unprofessional way out. I gave what came to me and this is why I'm so popular in Ireland, because I've also been proved right.

So, on my next trip to Northern Ireland I asked how Shan (pink and blue hair, piercings, tattoos) did with the really good horse? The one I'd said could go to HOYS.

Chris and Colleen said she'd shot it!

I couldn't believe it. I said, "She did what? Shot it? You're joking?" They said they couldn't believe it either. "Yeah, we knew you were bang on, but you see Shan is someone who won't let the horse go on somewhere and do better." I shook my head in disbelief.

So, I said, "Now you're going to tell me that the one that should have been shot, didn't get shot?"

They said, "No it didn't. It was put into a field."

On my third visit Chris and Colleen told me that the horse that hadn't been shot, had since been shot. When I asked why, they told me that a child had gone into the field and this bastard of a horse had attacked the child and had left the child badly injured.

I have no idea whether the child recovered, and I wish no ill of the woman I told that night to shoot her horse, but I would imagine she now wishes she'd done as I'd said instead of leaving it too late.

I don't take any pleasure that the horse proved me right, but it should never have been allowed to do so. I can only give what I am told. It is up to others whether they take any notice.

I remember when I'd first told her. Chris went, "Dear God, you're like a sledgehammer, you, aren't you?"

I know that sometimes when I get tired, I shouldn't say things like I do, but my readings are not about trying to be nice, they are about being honest – and sometimes that hurts.

CHAPTER 21

The Road Trips:
Orkney

I love going to Orkney and I've helped so many horses there. I remember on one occasion going into a stable block. I stood there with my back to the four horses that were in and said, with it all coming straight to me, "That little pony rolls off that heel, he's really sore on it, you're going to have him in trouble unless you do something about it."

The woman brought him out and said, "No, he's alright, but he is a bit stiff." I said, "Well, if you get that done, he'll be fine." And I asked her for a rasp. Once I'd got a rasp, I did his front feet. I said, "Now, watch him. Give him a few turns down there. Take him down the grass and on the concrete." It was as though I'd performed a miracle!

Sometimes the simple things I am told turn out to be the most believable for others. I know how hard it is to be told that you should shoot your horse. Who wants to hear that?

I've built up not just a reputation in Orkney but also very real, lovely friendships. It's like visiting friends, but everything still needs to be professional too.

I had a woman who fetched this horse to me and I said, "I don't like talking like this but I have to say what I am getting. I'm not here to insult you or embarrass anybody, but this horse is bored. You aren't doing enough with him."

Esme is such a great horsewoman and now runs the stables at Manor Farm.

Telephone readings now take up a great deal of my time at Manor Farm.

Watching for balance with farrier Lee Hardy.

Always time to get a fag on.

A chat of the mind with Freddie.

Coming down to see Royal MacNab and Freddie
every morning I'm home is an absolute privilege.

Alex is now working with me and has ambition.

Alex is enjoying being back with horses.

Alex on Last Encounter.

Whereas Eleanor likes being with wolves!

Eleanor recently came with me on my latest road trip to Orkney where the photograph here, used as the book cover was taken.

Back home on the farm with our goats.

Farrier Lee Hardy at work.

Sometimes I just don't know why I'm getting the messages that come, but I always tell it the way I'm hearing it.

Captain Mowbray & Me – this horse means so much in so many ways.

Royal MacNab.

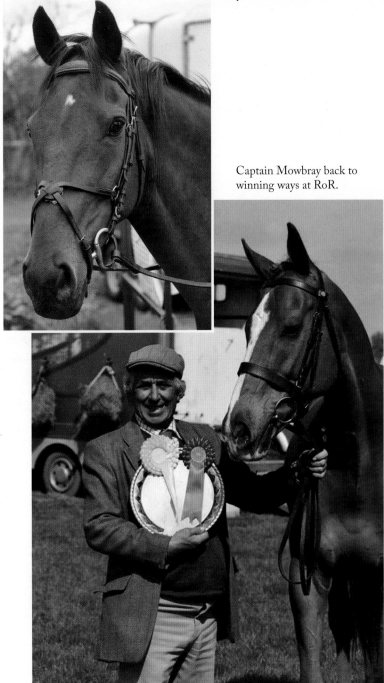

Captain Mowbray back to
winning ways at RoR.

Captain Mowbray.

I will always work with horses.

I didn't think she wanted to hear. She wasn't showing any interest, and then she said, "Well, I think you've got that wrong."

I always keep calm at this point, when it starts going this way. I waited a second or two, to help her, not me. Then I said, "That's fine, but nothing's written in stone, love. I haven't come with a script, that's what I just feel."

She said, "We ride out every day across the moors."

I said, "You're going the same way?" She said, "Yes. I go the same way every day." I asked how long she had been doing that for. "Oh, five years," she said. I said, "That's why he's bored. You're doing the work, but you're not expanding his mind. He's bored of it, seeing the same things. What a new environment will do, will be to give you and him that spur."

I think this woman was a bit offended by that. I was never going to go back on it. I never saw the bloody horse! It was around the corner, so I wasn't influenced by the horse maybe having its head down. It's what I had got off its mind. Think of it as though it was like you and me. Going the same way every day. How would you be?

I don't say what I say to offend anybody. Maybe once she'd thought about it, she took him a different way. I suppose I'll never know, but at least I told her what I'd been given.

Sometimes it's not just a reading that owners are after, it's because something is wrong, and they know it but they can't put their finger on it.

I was standing in the corridor of a stable. I can go to a yard and find the horse I am supposed to be doing the reading for by standing at the stable door or walking down and saying, "That's your horse," and people say, "How did you know that?" On this occasion I just asked, "Is he in the third or the fourth box up on the left?" I was told the third.

I said, "This horse is a nice willing horse with small levels of 'honest ability'." I never say minimal or little ability. I said, "He's lovely, but you need to relax on him a bit more, let him flow."

That's when she said, "What do you think to his feet?" I said, "His feet are fine." She said, "Well, you haven't seen them." I said, "I know, but I'm going on what I'm getting. His feet are fine. If I see them and change my mind, I'll tell you I'm wrong."

And then I said, "I tell you what, love, get him tacked up and bring him out and I'll show you exactly what I'm saying."

She was a really nice woman with a happy face. This kid brings the horse out and her riding instructor's standing there and the riding instructor said to me, "You know this horse is lame, don't you?"

I said, "He's not. Truly, I'm telling you, he's not."

Now I'm getting that this is the real reason I'm here, from their side. They want to know why he's lame because nobody can find the lameness. This is what happens.

I said to the kid, "Off you go and do what you would normally do." I was standing there with this riding instructor who I'm already thinking that she reckons she's just a bit good, because she's qualified and I'm qualified nowt, not a thing. Well, maybe fifty years of working with horses might qualify me a little.

The young girl on the horse brought him up to me. I took off the dropped noseband and I dropped the bit and then said, "Off you go again, but don't pick him up, don't take a contact, let him get his head out, squeeze him up with your legs."

But she was still riding off her hands. She was doing what the riding instructor would have told her to do. I said, "No, don't do that. Just drop your hands and give him some rein."

The owner was standing beside me and it was her daughter sat on the horse.

I said, "Just walk him round now," and she walked round three or four times. I then told her not to ask him to trot, because she kept gathering the reins up ready. I said, "Trot when I tell you to trot."

I'm now halfway through my fag I've rolled up while she's been doing this and the horse is loosened up. I knew this horse would be working on his memory if I wasn't careful.

I said, "Right. When you get down that long straight and you get to the letter B, I want you to ask him to trot, but I don't want you to touch his mouth and don't show him your reins. I just want you to let him travel up that long straight in his own stride."

Halfway up she wanted to grab him up. I shouted, "Don't you dare grab him up!" She trotted him up and around. I said, "Keep him going." And at that I saw the woman that owned the horse her daughter was riding with a tear running down her face.

I thought, "Oh, I've hit a nerve here, the right nerve." This horse is definitely sound, because if it wasn't it wouldn't be travelling like that.

I said to the woman's daughter, who was now doing really well herself. "Right, now pull it back to walk, change reins and do the same again.

I looked at the riding instructor and said, "The horse is not lame, love."

And to be fair to the riding instructor she said, "Well, blow me over with a feather, what have you done?"

I said, "That's my secret."

I tuned into the horse with reiki. I am a Reiki Master and that means that you don't need to use hands. It utilises the power of thought. That's why I hadn't wanted the horse to go back into its memory at that moment because it would have sent it back into its own ways and would have believed it was lame again.

If the girl had carried on the way she was going with the horse and not giving it chance to relax, it would then react and that's what would have caused it to look lame. I presume they'd had the vet in and the vet couldn't find the problem, but I went along and didn't listen to anything but what I was getting from the horse.

The tears of the owner and mother and the look on her daughter's face showed me I'd pleased them. The riding instructor was amazed. The horse wasn't lame. Job done. Next!

CHAPTER 22

Orkney:
Jimmy & the Spirit of the Old Man

I've just been back to Orkney this year in late July. A lovely woman called Kayte Prentice arranges my road trips there and I was absolutely made up that my daughter Eleanor came with me. We had a fantastic four days.

Eleanor is an outstanding young lady with a brilliant future ahead of her and she finally got to see me doing what I do; and what a stunning place Orkney is, with its captivating natural beauty and its lovely people like Morgan and Shelly Vendy who we met and whose horse I described as a rough diamond.

I have some special memories of this latest trip, but one of my favourite stories of all came on another road trip to these islands. It's the story of Jimmy and the spirit of the old man.

When I'm up in Orkney I can sometimes see as many as 60 or 70 horses, but I don't believe I can help every single horse. Some are way beyond me being able to give them anything but a little comfort before the inevitable.

On this occasion I went up to see a little horse at 10.45 at night. Up there they say, "Whatever time he gets here, it'll be fine," so we get into this old cow byre with a tin roof on it because the old, tiled roof had long since gone. This building was like 300 years old, like one of those little croft things with a concrete floor. It was fecking freezing it was, and there were no lights.

This little woman sounded like she must have been in her late 60s although I could hardly see her to vouch for that any further. I'm telling her all about this horse and asking whether she understands? She says, "Ohhh, yes. The kids and I have had a lovely journey with him."

That's when I clicked that I was hitting on the horse's memories and I know there's more to this. She's telling me all about the fun she's had and the shows she's been to with him. I responded by saying, "Your loyalty's second to none."

She said, "How is he in his health?" I'd not seen him at all yet at that point.

Then I got this little feller, he must have been about 5ft 1, behind me.

I said to the woman, "Look, love, I have to listen to the gentleman stood behind me."

She said, "There's nobody stood there." And she put a torch on. I said, "No, this feller's on the other side and he used to own this place. You bought it off him. Well, actually, he died suddenly and you bought it off his family."

She said, "Oh, aye. He was only a little feller." And I said, "He's telling me there's nothing wrong with the horse, and I have to believe him, but he also tells me I can get him right. That's how it's coming across, he's saying, 'You can get him right,' and to ignore what I see.

"Now, you're going to have to tell me what you think's wrong with him, because obviously there's something wrong with him, but he's not letting me see it and if I see it, I might be frightened of what I see."

"Ooohh," she said. "The vets are coming to put him to sleep on Monday.

And I'm going, "Oh I don't think so love."

I've got this little old feller stood beside me now and the horse behind me. He's a little chestnut pony. He's about 12 years old and he's stood in the dark.

I said, "What has the vet said?"

A lot of people don't tell me a vet is involved because I should never get involved without the vet's consent, but a lot of people only tell me once I've finished my reading.

I don't worry about it, because I'm not there to criticise anybody. I'm there to try and make the difference and I am trying to be constructive for the good of the animal.

She reeled off a list. "Och, rotating pedal bone, laminitis, discs, vascular, nothing we can do."

So, I said, "Well there's nothing to lose and everything to gain. I'm going to go and look at him," so we went to look with the torch and I went, "Dear sweet Jesus and all the disciples."

And I said to this little guy who was somewhere. "Well, you're going to have to fettling well help me here, because this looks like a proper car crash." And all I got back was, "You can do it."

I looked at this poor pony.

This guy had abandoned me now, having told me everything was alright. Now it was all down to me. I thought, "For the love of God! I've been dropped right down in the deep water here. Still, it's a good job I can swim." The old feller was right though.

Now, if I'd not had the old feller there and had listened to purely what was there, before what I'd seen, when I eventually looked at the pony, I'd have said, "Let the vet put it down," but you've got to have faith in what you hear and what you're told.

It's such a wonderful thing – and that experience with the old man was nothing short of magical, spiritual – but yeah, it's so strange, you can't describe it and I would be the biggest sceptic around, if I didn't believe in what I do, but when it comes like that, well you know that what you have and what you do is very special.

I looked at this horse and thought fettling hell, but then I picked up its foot and everything became clear. I said, "Oh, I can sort this, love."

She was pretty fair taken aback and said, "Can you?"

I said, "I bloody well can."

I knew as soon as I picked the foot up what the problem was. I said, "Look, love, get on your Facebook straight away and tell somebody I want a farrier's knife and I want a rasp and I want it here by ten o'clock in the morning."

Then Kayte rang and said, "What are you doing now?" I said I'm coming back to see Jimmy tomorrow, it's very important that I do. I knew that if I didn't go back, then things might not go right, and the vets might have put him down. I was on a mission for this pony called Jimmy.

Kayte said that all of the other owners who I still had to see would be panicking that I would be going to miss them the next day and that I wouldn't be able to make the charity evening where I was speaking and doing more readings, that I do to raise money for Riding for the Disabled Association (RDA).

I said, "At the worst I may be 20 minutes late for the charity evening. I'll see everybody, I'll get to the charity evening and still catch my plane back to England on time, but I'm coming back to see Jimmy, no matter what."

I went back the next morning and sorted Jimmy out.

I don't wave a magic wand, doing what I do. I got his feet right. But it was meeting the spirit of the old man in the building that did it.

The fact that Jimmy is still alive now was not down to me,

but down to the miracle from the old man's spirit. I was just there in the right place at the right time for Jimmy.

I started at eight o'clock that morning, just so that I could get to Jimmy in good time. I saw another 25 horses that day, got to the event and did four hours on stage to raise money for the RDA. And I still caught my plane on time.

As I left the islands again, I thought about the fantastic hospitality I am always shown. I certainly always have a full tank of fuel to keep me going when I'm there. And I smiled, thinking about Jimmy and the spirit of the old man.

CHAPTER 23

Dealing with a Crowd:
The Woman Who Didn't Have a Horse

Most of my time is devoted to one-to-one readings between myself and the horse owner, but there are times when I'm 'the turn' for the night. I'm the guest speaker, talking about what I do and then actually doing it in front of all their eyes by giving out readings about the people who are there and their horses.

I enjoy them because they are all in aid of a good cause like Riding for the Disabled or the Air Ambulance and I'm doing more of those now too. I've done them in Orkney and in Northern Ireland but more recently, just after the lockdown was over from the pandemic, I was 'the turn' at a village hall in East Yorkshire.

The organisers had sold tickets with me as the main event and had raised a substantial sum. While that was nice to hear I didn't take it as an ego thing, far from it! I just thought that now the pressure was on!

I was never trained in this kind of thing, although thinking about it I have never been trained in anything, so I don't know why I was suddenly thinking I needed training. I've never gone in anywhere with a script. You can't, because you've no idea what's coming.

All I know is I have to give what I see, because that's the honest way and you've got to believe what you see, even when you might doubt it.

I lower my head before giving a reading. I'm just preparing myself and it preps the audience too. They hush. Sometimes you could hear a pin drop.

I know that in any room full of people there will be sceptics. When I first started doing this there were more of those than I get today. These days the people who come to see me are largely the ones that want to hear me and hear what I have to say. They come to see Cooper Wilson, but there are still some that are sceptics, which is okay, but then why come?

I pick up on the biggest sceptic in the room and let her think she's dictating and let her think she's making me look like a prat, but I never feel embarrassed because I always believe that the others watching and listening will see what's going on.

I'm in the moment. This sceptic is rattling on and I know they're going, "She's a twat" or words a bit like that, children. The sceptic burns herself out, usually because the power of the mind from everyone else is telling her they've all had enough. It's happening less and less now though.

The venue for this evening was Holme on Spalding Moor between Howden and Market Weighton. There were about 100 in and Yorkshire Air Ambulance were certainly going to benefit.

When it's an evening like this you're never sure what to expect because it's not like I have rolled up for people who have brought their horses along when I'm on my road trips. People are probably just expecting a bit of entertainment, a night out.

People were asking questions and I had a blonde girl with a bottle of wine who I just thought was going to start on something and at that point I was given a message about her and her horse.

I said, "You've got a chestnut horse, love. And it has a bad back. I'd get your vet to look at that."

She said, "Oh, my God." I told her, "You might need to either jab him with steroids or he might need keyhole surgery." She just sat there blown away.

There was a woman at the back and I thought, "Here we go, here comes trouble."

She said, "Where have you come from, how have you got to here?" I said, "I've come from the gutter, love." I thought, this conversation could get nasty. I knew that someone like her was a bunny hugger and that she wanted to try me out, to ask about my role as a knackerman. I could see it. But she hadn't got it in her. I said, "I'm a self-made man, I'm self-taught."

Another woman asked me a question and that led me away from the probable trouble causer. Then the blonde girl I'd told about her chestnut horse said, "I've got a question about my horse." I said, "You come and see me after this evening love and I'll give you your answer." She said, "But I want an answer now." She hadn't even asked her question, but I knew what she was going to ask.

I said, "No, it's not for public ears." I know that she knows and cares for her horse and wants an answer straight away. I know she already knows what to do, what's coming.

In a public meeting like that I can't say to her, "Your horse needs putting down," but I knew straight away that horse had to go. But if I'd said it in there I knew that would set off the bunny hugger at the back. I did tell the blonde girl, after the event.

The daftest of conversations I had that night was with a woman who I kept saying had a horse, and yet she kept saying she hadn't. When I'd finished she came to me and asked why I'd kept asking. I said, "Because you've got a horse." She said again, "I haven't, but I've got one on loan." I thought 'stroll on' and I said, "The horse doesn't know it's on loan, love. It doesn't know whether it has been sold or not. It just sees a new handler."

I then said, "I'm not going to say anymore now because it has been a good night, I've had four hours up here and you're not exactly speaking very coherently."

That's a nice way of putting over the state she was in by that time. I won't tell you what happened next, but let's just say this young lady wasn't very ladylike! I put it down to the village hall by then having been locked and a physical need she had at the time. I shall say no more!

Anyway, a few weeks later I had to go into North Lincolnshire for a yard visit. It had been very successful. The yard owners told me there was a woman bringing a horse. I'd just said that when it arrived not to take it off the trailer.

I got on with finishing the readings I'd been doing and I was picking up messages about horses that had died at the yard. This is what I was picking up spiritually.

Outside one stable, I said, "The pony in there isn't the only pony in there." They said it was. I said, "No, it's not, because the horse that was in there before died in that stable and it's still there." I asked whether that was right and they said it was.

Anyhow, this trailer pulls up and I looked at the woman and said, "Don't I know you? Weren't you at the Air Ambulance fundraiser?" In one hell of a state and not acting at all like a lady, I could have said. Totally smashed, I could have said. She said, "Yes, I was."

Rather than go over old ground about whether it was her horse or somebody else's, I said, "So, you've brought your horse to see me, have you?" She said, "It's not my horse." Unbelievable. Stroll on! Here we go. I said, "But it is your horse, love."

So, now we have everybody in the yard, about 12 others all around. It's another audience.

I'm standing in the car park with a fag on and telling everybody about this horse in the trailer. I'm telling her about this horse, its ability, that she must trust it, go with it. I said, "It will be a flyer, but you've got to be a brave jockey to ride it because you will have to be so accurate with its jumping."

I then said, "But before you do anything more, you need to get your blacksmith in and ask him to balance the forefoot. He just plaits a little which prevents the hindquarters from coming through correctly, so he's not tracking up right because of this problem with his front-off fore."

I said: "Let him walk off the trailer and walk around." She walked him away and back and there was everyone there and they could see he was dropping his off fore. I said, "Because he can't extend through the shoulder, the back end can't come through, he's shortening behind."

I said, "You can't take the inside wall off but what you can do is get your blacksmith to put a quarter wedge on to balance him, to level him up and then his back end will move properly."

That's when she told me he'd just had surgery. I asked her what he'd had surgery on.

"The vet said it was his suspension," she said. "So, they've de-nerved him behind."

Now we were getting somewhere. I said, "Right, so that's why he can't feel his back legs are wrong, because there's no feeling to them."

I said, "I'm not saying this to insult anybody, but the horse is going to be no better for it, and you need to get that foot sorted."

She then said, "I wish I'd spoken to you that night because he was only operated on three weeks ago." I said, "Well, when I said you had a horse, I knew there was something to tell you and that's why I kept saying you had got a horse, love."

CHAPTER 24

Hartlepool:
Amazing Messages

What comes to me isn't in my power. I'm just the messenger. I can't tell you from one minute to the next what messages I'm going to receive, whether they are going to tell me something is wrong, something that happened in the past or how a horse might work or perform in the future.

I'm there because people want the readings. They want to hear. Sometimes they don't like what they hear, but I can't do anything about that. I'm really not in control, and if I was, I wouldn't be giving messages properly. I'd be a fake. You really must give what you see, like the old man in Orkney; or like persevering with the woman that had a horse but said she hadn't.

A shorter road trip, to Hartlepool, had seen me already having given readings on eight horses in this yard, after having given another ten earlier in the day near Sedgefield.

Sarah, who owns the yard is alongside me. I'm pretty much finished for the day. I've done all that has been asked of me. It has been an average day, nothing astounding. You get those. The readings are easy, there's nothing coming particularly dramatic.

There's a ten-year-old girl and her mother in the yard. The little girl is on this pony and something just comes to me as I'm on a fag, relaxed from the readings.

I said to Sarah, who is a proper North-East, no-nonsense

lass, "What I've got here is not really relevant to today's horses I've seen, but I have to say it."

And I told her about the pony this little girl was on. I said, "He truly appreciates you and thanks his lucky stars that he found you. He's had a very near, close-to-death experience and feels very lucky to be here. He nearly bled to death, he got very anaemic and very weak."

Sarah went as white as dust. She went into what I call proper Geordie, but Sarah will probably say it's proper North-East because Geordie refers to nearer Newcastle.

"F*** me," she went. "How the f*** did you know that?"

I said the pony had told me, that I was just the messenger.

The mother and the child didn't know about it. I said to Sarah, "Did you know?" She said, "Aye it had to be put on a drip, transfusion. It had been gelded, but gelded badly."

I told this little girl that she was really lucky to have come across him and he was really lucky to have her. I said, "He feels like you're a present to him."

I then told her, "You'll do really well with him, but what I don't want you to do is sit on his back and be twining." Her mum said, "Is he that clever that he knows?" I said, "Yes, he's sensitive. He feels he's doing the best he can and when your daughter gets upset, he gets upset too, because he doesn't know what he's done wrong, so she mustn't confuse him because it will unbalance him."

I said to the girl, "You're old enough to know what I'm saying, and if you argue with your mum in your own little whiny way when you are on him it affects the pony's spirit."

The little girl's mum was absolutely made up with what I'd said. What I hadn't known was the girl had artificial legs. I'd just presumed that because she was only ten years old her legs were maybe a little weak.

All of those words were just given to me. I didn't know what the purpose of receiving the messages was going to be, but they made a mum and her daughter very happy, and probably created an even stronger bond with the pony than before.

That's where my work, my spiritual guides, what people call the heebie-jeebie stuff, all makes sense, even if it is hard for people to believe.

And that wasn't all that day. And if that last one is hard for some to believe, try this.

I was with the owner of this next horse and it was down where they shower the horses.

I said, "This horse is a reincarnation of your old horse." The lady owner looked at me as though to say, "What?"

I said, "When you lost your old horse this horse would have been conceived and the map was already written out from that day on."

I told her everything about the old horse and the new one and I said that if she let him work and made him think that everything was his idea that he would be fantastic, but otherwise he would be a bit of a destroyer. She said, "Yes, he gets anxious."

I said, "If you let him think he's done everything himself, that everything was his own idea, he'll do really well for you."

I said that I couldn't tell her anymore, because that was all I had, but that this horse had been put there purposely for her.

She had just wanted to know whether or not she was doing the right thing. She hadn't expected me to say anything about reincarnation.

Funny old days, but I give what I'm told.

CHAPTER 25

Wetherby & Wakefield: Connemaras & Appaloosas

The messages I get are never wrong, it's just sometimes how I've interpreted them and how I have then conveyed them to others that has made them appear wrong. I'm only human, and human nature has such a way that you can get carried away with what you're given, and that can sometimes make you look stupid if you've not had the right life experience to cope with it.

Fortunately, I've had enough life experience to cope when things do take a little turn.

I remember the time I went to Wakefield and I was sitting in this yard on a bale of shavings. I had a woman to my left and a woman to my right. We were talking about this horse.

I'm giving what I'm getting, that the horse has a good understanding and a good relationship with both riders. He's a true gentleman. He doesn't rush, doesn't panic, feels no pressure, a thoroughly enjoyable nag who gets just enough attention to keep his balance right.

Then I said, and this is what turned out to be me almost hanging myself in their eyes, "If you were to say to me what breed did I think it was, I would say a good honest genuine Connemara."

The one to the right was a nice woman but started to laugh. She said, "You'd better come and have a look at him."

When she opened the stable door I said, "What a nice horse …" and I paused. "But nothing like a Connemara. Wow, he's an old chaser, isn't he?" She said, "Yes he is, a long way from a Connemara."

The other one was enjoying this now. "Connemara!" I could hear them saying, like two little schoolgirls.

I laughed along with them and said, "Bloody 'ell, what a turn up I am," and one of them said, "Yes, what a fettling waste of time."

That's when I turned serious and I said, "Woah! Half a minute, love …" She wasn't having any and said, again, "Well, he's no Connemara." I said, "No, he's not love, but you want to pat yourself on the back."

She said, "What for?" I said, "For making such a good job of a horse that has a mindset as honest as a Connemara. That's what that is. That's what I was being told, which is why I said what I said. You can't tell me he's not genuine, like I was telling you before you showed me him."

She said, "Yes, he's as honest as a day is long." I said, "And that's a Connemara."

They might have had a laugh over the way it came out, but they booked me for another reading three weeks later.

When the woman rang, I joked that she was the one with the Connemara that wasn't. I complimented her again, but then she said, "But you missed his kissing spine."

I said he hasn't got a kissing spine. She said, "No, he hasn't. He's had surgery for it." Stroll on! I said, "Well, then, he hasn't got a kissing spine that I missed, has he?" Honestly, some people just love thinking they've got one over on you.

I said, "How long is it since he had surgery?" She said, "Ten years ago." Ten bloody years, for heaven's sake and sweet baby Jesus!

Sometimes you just can't help people.

This one really makes me shake my head even now.

I went to a job in Wetherby. I'd had a busy old fortnight of non-stop readings, which really is mentally and physically draining. I was tired, but I'd got there and had met a woman who greeted me with the words, "Everyone in the yard thinks I'm completely stupid getting you."

I said that we could do it in the car park away from the others.

I said, "Being there in the yard, if they all have sceptical eyes I'll feel it and it can get in the way. Negative energy, it might spoil it."

I set off with my first reading and said, "I'm getting that there's no reason to fear this horse. He's really trusting." And immediately she said, "No, totally the opposite."

I stopped and said to myself, "Oh," but then I thought, "No, it's what I'm getting. I'm not going to back out of this. So, I thought, right, I'll go in from another message I was getting.

I said, "Right, he's a nice big bay horse, isn't he?" And she came back immediately again. "No, he's Appaloosa."

At this point I thought, "Well I'm getting this is a bay horse and I'm really not going to take much more of this," but I tried with another message.

I said, "Is he about 15.3–16.1 hands?" And she said, "Well, that's a bit average, isn't it?"

That was it for me. When she said that I thought my gasket had just gone, but she didn't know it. I just said, quite calmly, "I tell you what we're going to do madam. I'm calling it a day."

She said she didn't know what I meant.

I said, "I'm not taking this reading any further because everything I've said, you've said is wrong. Now what I see is a big, lovely bay horse that's kind and you've no reason to be feared of and he hasn't got a measuring stick so he can't tell me whether he's 15.3–16.1. I just see a big, solid, really good horse."

She said, "I'm not paying you for that."

Stroll on, again. Some people really don't have a clue.

I said, "I don't want your money, but what I do want to do is go and take a look at it," and she said, "Yes, you can see it."

She was that cocksure of herself. We walked down the yard and as soon as I saw it I said, "He doesn't look like an Appaloosa love, he's a dark bay. He's got a dark bay head, dark bay neck and he has a blue rug on, so I see the dark bay. He may have Appaloosa in his bloodline, and he may be an Appaloosa, but look at him. He looks like a dark bay."

She persisted and was now extremely put out. She said, "He's Appaloosa, and frankly I'm a little bit long in the tooth for all this s**t." Sorry, children.

I said, "I'm way too long in the tooth to put up with this. There's nowt wrong with that horse, love," and I walked off.

This job isn't all about perfection. It's about getting as close to the truth as you possibly can.

CHAPTER 26

Telling It Like It Is:
Back in Northern Ireland

I once went to see this pony owned by an English woman in Northern Ireland. We were going up the driveway towards this yard and I said to Colleen, "This is going to be a carry on," because when I'm not driving I can tune in to where I'm going. I can know what's coming and I knew this was going to be a bit of a bugger.

When we got there I was telling this woman that she had a good horse, so long as she gave it the belief that it was good. Her words about her own horse weren't complimentary at all.

She said, "He's a total bastard, he is."

You see, that's the reason I was getting that she had to give her horse belief, something good, a pat on his mane. Let him know.

I said, "You've been hunting on this horse though?"

She said she had, but that he hadn't been very good. I could only give what I saw. The horseman in me saw a horse that had done his job.

I said, "He looks like he's had a good day to me."

She wouldn't have it. She said he was very naughty. I thought to myself as we left, that at least she had toned down her feelings about the horse from bastard to naughty, so maybe I had done him some good and she might respect him a little more for the work he was putting in, which she wasn't seeing. So far as I was concerned she was all for going out riding, but not respecting her horse.

As we were driving out, Colleen said, "She goes hunting with that horse twice a week." I said, "Well, if he's that naughty, why does she take it?"

All she wanted from my visit was to have nice words said about her, not her horse. To my mind she didn't care about it enough, but maybe that change of mindset in the word she used about him at the end might have done her some good – and the horse too.

Like I always say, I'm there for the horse first.

I had another 'tuning in' as we approached the next yard and I said to Colleen, "If we get here and we get a dapple grey I can guarantee you it is fettling dangerous."

She said, "Oh, really?" I said yes, "It wants a bullet."

When we arrived I was introduced to a nice couple and the first thing I saw was a brown horse. I didn't see a grey at all during the readings.

I got to the stage where there was just one more to do and the man from the couple said, "It's just around the corner." And there it was, a grey 'un.

I was steadying myself and about to be diplomatic about it because of what I was building up to saying.

Colleen was looking at me and she said, "Just tell him what you told me in the car." I said, "I don't know whether they can take the truth or not."

The couple were both there. I said I had got information about this horse before I even got to the yard. The feller said, in his broad Irish accent, "Well, just fettling tell me then, don't go hanging aboot boring the fettling shite out of me."

I still wasn't convinced they were ready for this, for me, some feller from Yorkshire who'd never seen them and their grey horse before, maybe never would again and I'm telling them to destroy a horse.

I mentioned about putting on the kettle. I was still being diplomatic, but this feller wasn't having any of it.

He said, "What are you going to tell me about the grey horse?" I said, "It wants a bullet.' He said, "Too right it does."

After he'd said that I explained why I'd not come right out with it. I said to him that I have to be so careful, but he said, "Well, that's the way I like you to speak and the way I like to hear things."

At that I jokingly said, "I've bored you witless then? (It was a different word to that one, yes). He said, "Too fecking right you have, but you were right about them all, including the grey." All he wanted was confirmation he was doing the right thing.

Irish people want the truth, straight at them, between the eyes, doesn't matter how hard it is.

What I say when I go out anywhere now is that I'm not in control of what I'm saying. I believe in what I see or what I am told, and I say it even if it sounds stupid. There's a purpose for it being said. Which brings me to my next story.

I went to Ireland when the pandemic was on. I didn't break any restrictions. I just went at the time when I was allowed to go.

There had been a good number of horses that had been brought into this yard. A pony came in. I didn't know who the woman was that was with her. I was telling her about the pony. There didn't seem a lot to say as there was not a lot going on in any messages. The pony was confident. It had a bit of faith in itself and was a good leader. I told her all this and then I asked if she had any questions.

At around that time there had been a little girl killed up the road from me on a pony in England and I'd thought that the little girl that I now felt stood alongside me in Ireland was her.

But thought and the spirit world are two very different things. There's a saying 'You know what thought did,' and I know how that can be attributed to this story because in the spirit world things come to you without thinking.

I was looking at the horse. It was big. And I'm looking out on to a green bank, a grass hill field.

That's when I said, "This horse has not had a good experience, has he? Would I be right in saying the little girl stood beside me is the one that suffered?"

The woman was visibly shaken. I could see the look in her face. This was hurting.

It then clicked. This girl was not the English girl that had lost her life, this girl had been riding this pony. I'd seen it because of looking out at the hillside. I said, "This girl got killed," and we went on from there.

I did the woman more good than I did for the pony on that day. This woman had been the riding teacher of the girl that had got killed and this girl that I'd had next to me was that girl. The teacher had a really bad conscience over it. My words at least brought some comfort for her. She couldn't believe it.

And off Colleen and I went to the next one.

At the next yard I told the owner about her grey horse. It had a swelling on the leg, but I'd said that he could still go and do a job. He had the lifestyle he wanted. Happy days.

I then gave a reading for the one opposite him. And this time I didn't mess about. Maybe I had the Irishman's words from the couple I'd been with earlier still in my ear, to get straight to the bad news.

I said, "I'm going to say about something here," and I could feel Colleen going, "Fecking hell, here we go again." I said, "Take that around the back of the building and knock it on the head," and the owner said, "Why?"

I said "It's dangerous, love, because it can't see what it's doing. It's blind or short-sighted and that makes it very dangerous." She said, "It'll break my daughter's heart." I said, "It's better than putting her in a wheelchair."

After getting over the shock, she said, "I won't be taking it around the corner. I'll be putting it on a meat wagon, that'll be sure. At least then I'll be for getting something out of it!"

That's how blunt the Irish like you to be, and how they deal with things.

CHAPTER 27

All Horses Have Potential:
From Beef or Salmon to the Best They Can

Every racehorse owner wants a Gold Cup or Derby winner; every three-day eventer trainer wants a Burghley champion; and right down to a local level we all want to have a horse that gives its best whether for happy hacking or whatever.

I believe all horses have potential, it's just that all horses are not created equally in terms of their ability to go fast, jump high and their stamina. Just like humans you can achieve over and above a level through the right exercise, diet and training, but I also believe you can do so much more with a horse if you understand its ways, its moods, the things that make it tick.

And everyone wants to know, from me, what I'm getting from each horse. Some like to try out my sensory perception, just to see how accurate I can be at working from very little information.

It can happen as simply as this. I'll be sitting at the kitchen table of a yard and I'll be given a headshot of a horse either in a photograph or a screen shot on a mobile phone. Then I will be asked to tell about the horse.

This happened on one occasion in Northern Ireland.

I looked and then said, "He'll dig deep when he has to, takes life in his stride, but knows who he is, knows he's successful." I got that he was a jumper, but I hadn't got racing. I said, "He's a good jumper, but by God he does dig deep and sometimes if he says no, that's it. He's honest and he's a true gentleman, but by God has he got some health problems due to his work."

I don't always see horses racing and it is impossible to know every horse, and I certainly hadn't come across him previously. I also know that some racehorses don't even know they are racehorses.

I said, "As far as I'm concerned, he's now just an old pointer or a good fun horse that's won a race or two, but I don't see the racehorse in him – but I do see the point-to-point horse in him."

I said, "One thing is for sure and that is that he's proved himself. He's never been a bragger and now he's perfectly relaxed and laid back about life. He doesn't need to prove anything and these days he thinks I'm not bothering. On those days in the past when he needed to dig deep he achieved a lot."

This owner was amazed. He said, "You don't know who or what the horse is?" I said, "No."

It was a horse called Beef or Salmon and he'd finished fourth in the Gold Cup! It wasn't a bad reading considering all I had to go on was a photograph. I just thought he was an old pointer but that's the mindset of the horse. He probably never saw himself as a racehorse.

He was then 14 years old and peacefully retired. He'd done everything that had been asked of him and I could see he didn't want to put heart and soul into it any longer. It was such a laidback fulfilled horse and that's what I'd been getting. It was wonderful.

The next day the owners took me to the local pub where Beef or Salmon had been named and where the syndicate had been put together.

But sometimes horses don't achieve anywhere near their

potential because owners and trainers don't get to know their horses and what it is that gives them their spark.

I was over in East Yorkshire and was standing with this lady owner who asked about her horse.

I said, "This horse is an old racehorse and he's holding on to those memories." Sometimes I can get the age. I thought this one was about 15–16. I said, "He hasn't done much since he came out of racing. He's just enjoying life."

The lady owner was fascinated by what I'd said and asked me a similar question to the one when I'd found out later it was Beef or Salmon. She said, "Do you think he was a good one?" I said, "I can't tell you different to what I'm getting, that he thinks he's done his job the best he can."

She said, "Well, he was at the back each time and they just gave up with him after a couple of runs."

I said, "The problem is that they didn't ask him to try and better himself, so he's done what he thinks was right. Out of the back door that's a racehorse." She said, "Yes, he used to enjoy his racing. But just wasn't fast enough."

I said, "But he needed chucking in at the deep end. This one has been wrapped in cotton wool. Nobody has sat there and said bang-bang, let's go with him. After so many runs jockeys know what's what and they are inclined to sit horses like this out and see what happens, so the horse gets a bad reputation, but I'm telling you this horse felt he was doing well."

And that was why he was contented in the same way as Beef or Salmon because although he's never risen to Beef or Salmon's heights, he'd felt satisfied, because nobody had tried hard enough to see what more there was in him.

Back in Northern Ireland again, and I won't give this lady's name because she's quite famous, even though I didn't know who she was at the time. I was visiting again to do a reading.

I said, "This horse isn't at the top yet." Quick as a flash she came back with, "It is." I said, "It doesn't think it is. This one knows what it's doing but doesn't feel it has achieved its best yet. I see it doing better."

She said, "No, it's at the top." I then tried to get an idea of what she considered to be the top. I came up with the heights of the fences. It was a show jumper. I said, "What's up with your 1.55s then?" It turned out it had only been doing 1.40s. She said, "It's not at 1.50s yet." I said, "Well, you're not at top yet, are you?" I said, "This horse will get you there, but just one thing more, don't tell it what to do or else it'll tell you where to go."

I could see what sort of character it was, and it was a brilliant horse. I've since watched videos of it in action over 1.60s, and stroll on, it really has fulfilled the potential I saw in it that day.

I spoke to a woman in Tipperary who had a grey cob. It was a phone reading. I said, "I can see you at the very top of your tree, being very successful with this grey cob you have."

She said, "Oh, I don't know." I said, "There's nothing wrong with him that a good diet won't keep right. He's so willing to give everything."

And he did just that. Over the next three years this horse was Supreme Champion at HOYS (Horse of the Year Show, for those who don't know) and at Royal Dublin – and she had doubted it.

This same lady had another horse, a chestnut. I said, "He's a good horse but he needs time, don't push him as he's underdeveloped." She said, "He looks alright, but I haven't got time to do him."

That was the point at which sometimes it's not what you know but who you know, and I knew exactly the people that could nurture this animal, let it achieve its potential. Colleen and her family.

Fortunately, this lady knew them too and was immediately receptive.

I had said, "Send him to somebody that's got time, but send him to the right people – and I know who." At that moment I didn't know she knew Colleen.

Colleen sent me a video, sometime later, with her daughter Shireen on this horse, without mentioning anything other than, "What do you think to this horse?"

I didn't put two and two together, but I did say, "Oh, give him time, he's a real machine, he'll be a world beater."

I think they ended up taking a serious amount of money for him. Colleen had listened to me in giving him time and by heck did he come out of his shell!

These are just a few of those readings either on the phone, in a stables yard or on individual farms and homes that I conduct every day of the week.

Some people want to see if I can find out where they are going wrong. A lot of people have got horses or ponies for hacking and just want to do right by their animals. Others have horses and want to know what kind of potential they have. They are all horses to me, all with their own personalities, traits and abilities.

When I give readings there is now a general feeling of nothing to lose and everything to gain amongst owners and trainers.

If I see a defect or something that appears wrong with the animal, then I tell them, that's all. If they want me to help in some way, I'm happy to work with the horse.

I ask whether there are any questions, as sometimes owners

are curious about what else they can do to make their horse happy, but often they'll go, "No, you've answered them all."

And that's good. I like working with people who love their horses.

CHAPTER 28

Emotional Decisions:
When It Is Time to Let Go

One of the most delicate times is when I am asked (often these are on the telephone for obvious reasons) to conduct readings for old or very poorly horses. It is always important for me give the reading properly, from what I am being given spiritually, but it is also important to be sensitive to the emotions the owner is feeling.

I was conducting a reading for a woman on the telephone who was taking her horse to the vet and she wanted to know what she should do. She said there was so much else going on in her life that she'd lost her way with what to do. Sometimes people do that. They then start overthinking a problem that sends them round in circles or they get into a rut and don't know how to get out of it.

This is when people going through this kind of thing pick up the phone and ring me, because I'm looking from the outside in. But I'm not getting information from the person, I'm getting what the horse is going through. That way you can help that person come out of a rut. You can get them out of the rut and they can go forward.

This woman didn't know what to do.

I said, "I am really sorry, but there's nothing I can do to help the horse because I have missed my opportunity to try and make a difference."

I then described her grandma to her, and she said, "Yeah." And then I said, "This horse stands in a corner box, doesn't he?" She said, "Yeah," again. I said, "When you have him put to sleep he will come back to that box because that's where he feels safe." She said, "Yes, he does, he feels safe in the stable because when he's out he's in so much pain and discomfort."

Then I got something else that came to me, there was something else there, so I said, "Right. You've a flower vase, it's completely opposite to anything else, it doesn't match anything." She said, "I can't think of anything. Oh, I have, it's down by the door." I said, "It's multicoloured, but I see greens and blues." She said, "Yes, it's mainly green and blue with tinges of gold and yellow in it." I said, "That's your grandma who is telling me what's in your house and that what I'm saying should be believed."

Then I told her, "The journey you've been on has been an experience that nobody could ever have paid for. What you've got to take out of this disappointment is the joy you've had with him (her horse). It's not about you letting him go and feeling you have done him wrong. You would feel wrong if you didn't let him go. What you've got to do is take the good out of your experience and not feel guilty about what you have to do because when that man up there shouts for that card there's not a man in the world can help you."

I knew the horse was knackered and I could understand that the vets were saying they could try this or that, with all good intent for the woman, but I could see it was throwing good money after bad.

I never saw the horse. That woman messaged me later. Now at peace. The evidence I gave her helped that woman make that very difficult decision. That's the honesty.

Another woman, this time on the south coast, rang me out of the blue. She asked whether I needed her to send me anything. People are constantly amazed when I say no.

I said, "Don't bother, my dear. It's universal energy, the guardian angels, spirit guides that want you to have the information for this horse, so that you can do right by it."

I didn't call what her horse had, as being a kissing spine because that's diagnosing. I said, "It's got a restriction to the vertebrae and it's got an inflamed spinal cord."

That's what I was getting, all to do with spiritual energy. I said, "I will tell you now, whatever you do for this horse you will not be helping it."

Now I wasn't telling her outright to put the horse to sleep, but the information I gave her should have brought her to that decision. There was nothing to be done.

Apparently, I found out later, everybody had been approaching the horse and saying it looks like this or that. They were working off an opinion, but I work off what is right, even though giving the words given to me spiritually is hard to believe for many.

But let's now give the other side of the coin to those two stories. I get the messages the other way too.

I had been sent to put down a horse at a place in Harwood Dale near Scarborough.

It wasn't meant to be a reading, but the sprits interceded. Driving over I kept getting the message, 'Bullet's the lazy way out.' I asked the spirits, "If that's the case, tell me about the horse."

I was still getting that same message when I arrived at this really posh place. Everything was very smart, clean and almost clinical.

When I got there, I spoke to the lady owner and said, "I don't know if you know what I do, but I have to share this information with you. And it has made me very nervous about this. I believe putting the horse to sleep is the wrong thing to do."

She said, "The vet told me it was all we could do." I said, "No disrespect to your vet but the problems aren't in the feet, they are in the way it's shod."

Its shoeing had been incorrect. It was a big, very talented bay horse that had never had chance to prove himself because he had always had these problems.

Again, I hadn't seen the horse at that point. This is what I had been given spiritually. I said to bring him out and when she did, I said, "I'm sorry, love. If you want this horse put to sleep you will have to get somebody else to do this, because it's against my belief to put down a good horse. I can get this horse right."

She asked what I would do, and I told her. I said that blacksmith Danny Bentley would sort it for her. Danny did what I said. He put a little wedged heel on with a pad. That horse had another nine years and it achieved what it wanted, both going hunting and cross country. It was one of the most enjoyable spiritual experiences of my life.

CHAPTER 29

Reiki:
The Distant Energies

When I am booked to visit for readings, I will often use Distant Reiki. It's all about connecting our energies that make us all up whether humans or animals. It's a universal energy with the spirit world. I ask the spirit world to take the reiki energy that I can give, surround the horse with it, allow it to relax in its mind so that I can get into its subconscious mind.

I used it recently in Liverpool. I was at a yard and I was standing around a corner from the stables, talking to the owner and said we should go get a brew. We sat on a bench and I had a fag while we drank our tea.

At that point I'd caught a glimpse of this horse and held on to the connection, that energy. When we'd finished, I said, "Your horse will have his head down now." And she said, "Aye, he's tired."

As we walked closer to the horse, she then looked a bit more curious, "Oh, he looks very drowsy." I think she was a bit worried, but I let her know that he was that way because of the reiki I'd used distantly to get him relaxed. He was now well chilled out.

I know it can be a bit spooky, but it works.

Sometimes, if I just go into a yard the horses there can feel it and will just lie down or stand with their heads down, ears dropped, lips dropped, just relaxed. That is the power of reiki healing.

Spiritually I can go in to see a horse and immediately say he's got a problem in say his lumbar 3.

This is just an example. Say he's got polar pressure, which is at the back of the head. How I work with reiki close up is that I feel red heat and stuff and will then put my thumb in a specific place and I'll hold it there.

Within a short while of applying the pressure I'll wipe him clean and ask the owner or groom to walk him out. I have lost count of the number of times I've heard the line that goes something like, "How on earth did you do that?" as the horse walks out freed from pain.

Wherever I go my intention, through being led spiritually and through my own knowledge as a horseman, is to find out if the horse is walking pain free, if he is happy in his work, and what can we do to make him feel happier if he's not. It's then not how much I say, but what I say and do that's important.

I am always led by the spirit world or the guardian angels, wherever I go, to give me the information that's necessary for the quality of life for this animal that I'm going to see. Sometimes those messages just come. They are there. Sometimes I ask, and whenever I do, I will always get what is necessary.

CHAPTER 30

The Horse That Married Its Owner

I receive some absolutely mind-boggling messages, things that I don't understand, but that often start making some form of sense when I tell an owner.

I've said once or twice in this book, that if I hadn't experienced all of the things I have with the spirit world, going right back to the stag, and if I hadn't been able to help the thousands of horses and people I have, I would be just like some who will always be cynics.

And this message is certainly right up there in the 'this bloke's a nutter' territory when you hear what I said at first, except in the end it really did make sense.

I was conducting a reading somewhere in Lancashire when this message came to me about this lady's horse. I couldn't believe it, but I had to give her what had come to me.

I said, "Excuse what I'm going to say, but did you get married to this horse? Because I'm getting this information." I'd heard somewhere that some people feel married to their dogs, so I just said it as I saw it.

She took it well enough, given that it was a whacky thing to say, and just said, "No, I didn't get married to it." I said the rest of what had been sent to me, "I see you in a wedding dress." She said, "No, I got married in France, but what I did do when we came back was that I hired a castle and had a photoshoot."

We were making progress. I said, "But you didn't have your husband with you for the photoshoot?" She then said, "No. I had my photographs of me in my wedding dress, with my horse."

I laughed out loud. I said, "That's why the horse thinks you got married to him!"

That was such a lovely story, because it was important for her to know that he's got a memory of that. She took him to this photo shoot so she could get photos with him while wearing her wedding dress, so the horse thought he was at the wedding.

Okay, he didn't know it was a wedding, but her husband wasn't there dressed up, so he thought it was him and her!

I could have easily let that go, not told her because she might have thought what kind of doolally have we here, but what I give is the honest messages that I get coming through me.

When you get that kind of message you've got to question it. How the hell did I get that?

But obviously I got it because he's had that real experience, an experience he's had, enjoyed and is proud of it. It's amazing – and it still amazes me now.

The horse that married its owner! Well, I never!

CHAPTER 31

The Power of Newcastle Brown Ale

There are times when you can have all the horsemanship knowledge in the world, you can have all the spiritual guides too, but the one thing that makes all the difference is a good, plain and simple, old-fashioned remedy.

I had a woman on the phone from West Sussex. I had given her the reading about the horse she was concerned about and we were going through what I'd said again.

Some people listen, but they don't hear what you've said, so what I do is I go through it again with them. I walk them through what it all means, and we try to understand what the message might be, because the message isn't always clear. On this call I summed up what should be done by saying this was what she should do and I sent it to her in a text message. She replied saying, "I can't do that."

A few weeks later I received a message from the lady. I follow up, because I'm interested in how a horse is progressing and whether the people I have given readings to have taken up on what I've said.

On this occasion the lady in question had rung me – and I had no idea who she was at first, but she sounded in good heart.

She said, "Reluctantly, I did put him on that diet you suggested." I had said she should try her horse on Newcastle Brown Ale.

I said, "I tell you what. I bet you're laughing at those doubters right now, aren't you, because presumably you're ringing to say he is alright." She said, "Well, I'd never have believed it, but funnily enough he is."

I resisted the temptation of turning into a Geordie and saying, "Why-Aye!", and instead I just said, "It's funny what a bit of food does, love." We had detoxed it with Newcastle Brown because its bladder wanted flushing out.

She laughed herself then, when she said, "But, I've had to stop giving him it now, because he's flooding the stable out."

I said yes, but he needed it.

Forget the heebie-jeebies! There's a place for everything, including an old-fashioned remedy!

CHAPTER 32

Horses for My Irish Family:
Sixpence & Ben

Giving horses a good life, a better life, is what I live for. It makes me happy. It's what I've tried to do all my life, right from those days when my dad was a hunt servant, and I was working with those that were only one step away from being put to sleep.

Ever since my work with horses on behalf of the RSPCA had finished, I have been constantly approached by individuals and local authorities to help them and one such time came about when a tenant had been evicted at Whitby.

It involved 16 horses, all stallions barring three and was all handled under the Control of Horses Act. Because of the legal situation the landlord didn't want to be accused of taking horses for financial gain, so what he did was sell them all to me for sixpence each.

I bonded with one of the stallions a six-year-old that from what I had been able to work out must have spent the previous five years of his life more or less wholly in a stable.

I'd got his trust. The reiki had been helping, as well as messages I was getting about him and how to handle him. I called him Sixpence.

Once I'd broke him in as a stallion and seen he was controllable and level-headed, doing what was asked, he was a joy. It's a two-way thing. You have to adjust to the horse as well, make life easier for it, make each one content.

We then gelded him and after he got over his gelding we started working again.

It was at this point I realised that there was more of a good horse in there than I could get out of him, due to the level of work I have on, and the thing with my job is that you've got to know when you've done as much as you can.

I'm not saying I couldn't have done any more, it was purely down to not having the time available to give to him, and that's the time when you calculate that you are not doing the animal any favours.

But I know a very good family in Ireland. I would class Colleen, Chris, Chloe and Shireen, Chloe's sister, as my Irish family. Colleen arranges all of my road trips in Northern Ireland. I rang Colleen saying, "Does Chloe want to take Sixpence?"

Colleen took Sixpence on and his name now is Frazer. Together, Chloe and Frazer have won everything from show jumping to working hunter and show hunter and all at a very good level at about 1.10m.

It's not about getting the money, it's about me giving the horse a life. I gave the horse to them, they do enough for me. Coleen puts all the work in and whatever she gets is, in my book, very well earned. They are a wonderful family.

I wanted to give both Shireen and Chloe the best horses in the world, the best I could find. That was another pipe dream because they live a similar life to myself in that they are working-class people and don't ask anybody for anything.

Chris drives a horsebox for a living. He's never off the bloody road, but he's got dreams of wanting cattle.

Chloe is a wonderful horsewoman, the best in all Ireland so far as I'm concerned, but she just needed an opening and I hope

Sixpence or Frazer is giving her greater opportunities in bigger events. He even has a third name as Alex and Esme called him Red while he was with us.

Then there's Ben's story.

I used to go and see him at Addingham in West Yorkshire. I went to see him a few times and after the third time, I said to the lady owner. "You want to get some bloody work into this horse."

She was finding excuses not to ride him and was getting the vet involved because he had gone very weak. I knew why he was getting weaker. He wasn't working. She wasn't working him. He started showing lameness, his topline no longer able to carry the undercarriage.

I said to the lady, "I don't want to know what the vet has done. I'm only going on what the horse is telling me about itself and we need to have faith in that and not just the science (the vet's work)."

She seemed to go with what I was saying and then a short while later I received a text message that said they would like to gift Ben to me, because they knew I would do right by him.

I don't generally turn down offers as a rule because it can look like rejection, but I wasn't going to turn this offer down. I knew he was a lovely, big horse with real potential.

I said, "I'd love to take him." But at the same time I thought it would never happen because he's such a good-looking horse and someone would offer her some money and she'd be tempted.

Unbeknown to me, she had it all planned. "You can have him on 15 February, because I want to spend time with him before he goes."

I thought, "I'm missing something here, have I got this wrong?" I was trying to work out why she was giving him to me.

I couldn't work it out.

I can get messages nearly all the time and know exactly what's going to happen, but this one? It was a bit of a mystery.

This time all I was getting back was, "No, there's nothing wrong with him, he is just a lovely big horse." But still I was thinking, "I'm missing something here." I was then doubting what my spirit guide was saying, which is very unlike me.

I rang Colleen again and said, "I've got a lovely horse here, I just haven't got the time to put into him that I would like to."

I said, "I'd like the girls to have him." I knew that Colleen was looking for horses for both of them.

Shireen took him on and I said to Colleen, Chris and the girls, "For the first year just do show horse, nothing else, because he has been very weak and he's not up for the competitive jumping circuit yet. Take your time and get him fit and ready."

To buy a horse like Ben you'd normally need a lot of money. And in the first year they started showing him he won 12 show hunter classes, took 11 reserve championships and was a supreme champion all over Ireland.

Chloe is now jumping him and I just take pleasure on hearing how well they are doing. Ben has been to Balmoral and a few big shows, he's had a great time.

I went back over to Addingham more recently, to the same yard where Ben had been, to see this grey horse.

I was starting to get a similar feeling about this one that I'd had with Ben and so I said, "If you can't cope with this horse, send it to me," and someone in the small crowd that was there said, "Don't forget what he's done with Ben. If you let him have it, he'll do a better fettling job than you," but the owner was quite different, much more what you might expect, and said, "No, I'm never going to part with this horse," which was absolutely fine.

That was when I started tuning in to who was there. When the person had said what they had, I thought, what will I find out here? About Ben? There is a saying that, 'If you keep your mouth shut, you'll always hear more.'

I was interested because of what had happened, the way it had. It had always been a mystery to me. It hadn't stacked up. The bit about getting the vets in, but then suddenly taking my advice on, instead of the vets' words. It had been a bit too easily done.

I thought that maybe I would get to know the truth.

The person who had just sung my praises, probably the owner of the yard, then said, "We know he's in Ireland. We thought he was coming to you to be put down because of the cost of euthanasia through the vets."

I'd found the real reason she had suddenly gifted him. My spirit guide had been right. There had been nothing wrong with that.

I was told the reason she was getting rid was because she and her husband were getting divorced and she needed every bit of money she had, not to throw it all away on having a horse put to sleep.

So, all this flannel about, "We know you'll do right by him, was really all about being the cheap option. However, it could have been idle gossip. It didn't matter of course, and everything worked out for the best – and my spirit guide had been right all along!

CHAPTER 33

A Message from Tim:
Pip

As well as working with horses to improve their wellbeing, make them feel good, I am also a man who puts them to sleep. Nobody likes the job. Somebody has to do it, and I have done it since I was helping my dad. I don't do it much now. I do it when I'm asked, for people who know that I will do it right.

The role still has that unfortunate name 'the knackerman', but it is a job that is needed in the horse world.

One morning in 2018 I got a call from my friend Liz. "We're going to have to call it a day with Pip," she said. "We have exhausted all options." She asked if she could bring Pip to me, to be put to sleep.

But there was a part of me that wasn't convinced it was Pip's time to go, but I reserved my judgement as I knew that Liz was a very experienced horsewoman who would have tried everything before contacting me.

We organised for Liz to bring Pip and throughout the week leading up to Pip's arrival I was constantly being made aware that it was not Pip's time. The message was, "Science cannot heal the mind or the soul."

Pip arrived and as the horsebox was pulling into the yard I heard a whisper again, "It's not Pip's time to go, he will be going home." I asked where the information was coming from and the reply was, "It's Tim." Tim was Liz's late brother.

Tim gave me the reassurance to have faith in what I needed to do. "Don't be put off by what you first see," he said.

The top doors were opened and peeking just above the still vertical ramp were two little ears and a thick black mane. The ramp was lowered and there stood Pip, a bright-eyed bay pony with a stripe on his nose.

He stood alert, all 13 hands of him, but his body was riddled with hives, some the size of tennis balls, from his girth to his sheath. They were haematoma-like lumps. He came off the wagon eagerly and full of enthusiasm but clearly very uncomfortable.

Liz said her goodbyes and I took Pip into a stable. Normally I will leave a horse to settle, have some food and relax, but I decided to stay and I sat with him in the stable for well over an hour using reiki, and working out what I needed to do. It all became clear.

I sent Liz a text asking if she would allow me one last try. "Be my guest," was Liz's response. A sense of relief rushed through me.

I set about doing what I needed to do and two days later everything was as it should be, and the hives had completely disappeared. I didn't ring Liz immediately in case they reappeared, but I was confident they would not.

When Liz sent a text saying, "How's it going?" I replied, "You can pick him up on Saturday." Liz rang me. "Are you serious?" This wonderful horsewoman was full of emotion. "You're making me cry, Cooper, thank you!"

Liz picked up Pip and two weeks later he won the Trec championship and is still going strong today at 22 years old (2022).

All of science is amazing, the work that vets do is amazing, but in the equine world there is that need for treatment of the mind and soul – and that is what Pip needed from me.

CHAPTER 34

Horses in Rehab:
Manor Farm

When a horse comes here, to Manor Farm, nine times out of ten I will have already visited it and I will already have done 'the reading', so that when it arrives I'm already ahead of the game.

I've stabling for eight horses now, which allows for stabling of two or three of our own horses and capacity for the rehabilitation work. When I was doing the RSPCA work we had 25 horses here at any one time but this now works well for us.

We've had a lot here that have been under veterinary care and the vet has said, "There's no more we can do," and often the owner has come to me as their last hope, last chance saloon hoping I can help where others haven't been able to.

Of all the horses I've had in the last five years I have only lost one and in the past 18 months in the lead-up to this book I've had 40 that have either gone back to their owners or I have rehomed them.

Forget the readings now, forget what I call the heebie-jeebie stuff, forget all the bit about the stag. This is where the Yorkshire Horseman is very real, no readings, no wondering what all those messages are about for those watching. This is where the rehabilitation work is done.

I am a very lucky man, because I understand that I have the ability to give a horse a life, or give a horse its life back, and I know there cannot be many people that can do that. I want to give a life to every horse I come into contact with, which isn't always possible but where I can, I do.

Esme runs the yard and the bookings these days and she is a wonderful horsewoman. We work well together. Esme is really into rehabilitation work with horses and also, where needed, finding new homes for them.

I don't get anything out of it monetarily. That's not why I do it. I tell Esme what to do with each horse that comes. Once I've given my readings, and if I feel the horse would benefit from being at Manor Farm, I will tell the owner to get in touch with Esme, because she runs the yard and knows what's going on. Esme will then organise the detail over how much it costs to stable the horse. That's where Esme earns her wage.

But what I do is this. I put my effort in for the horse, not for anybody else. I don't do it for the owner. I do it for the horse, which is why I don't charge for what I do while the horse is with us.

And the horses that come here are not all older horses either. In more recent times we've had a little black and white mare called Mary who came in. Mary had been struggling for nearly a year. She was from near Pocklington.

As I was driving over, I had all the information I needed, before I'd even arrived, because I'd tuned into its environment and because I was asking for information to help the horse.

I said to the lady owner, who said she'd had all the experts in, "You've been treating the obvious and not the cause."

She brought it to me a few days later and I had Mary sound within a week. It was all down to my farrier, Lee Hardy.

We trimmed the foot, but it wasn't a conventional trim, it was a trim to help the limb, as I'd told Lee, who did as I'd asked, as it was the opposite to what you would have thought to do.

What they had been doing with Mary was they had not been treating the cause, which was coming from the foot, but another foot.

The obvious, that they had been treating for, had been a swelling on her hind leg, which they had tried to treat with laser treatment, but she wasn't walking properly on her off hind and that was because they had taken that support piece away.

The owner couldn't believe it.

I'd treated the cause, which was the foot, but it hadn't been the foot that the experts had been working on. We got this lovely, friendly little mare back going again and we sold it, on the previous owner's behalf, to a little girl up at Richmond. Everyone's happy, but most of all for me, the horse, who now has a lovely home and is doing a fantastic job.

We had a horse come called Headstrong Harry. I'd been over to see this lady owner about a year before. She asked me to go back to take a second look. He'd lost condition and didn't look good. She'd said that his behaviour was bad, which is why we gave him his name when he came to us.

I had previously told her, when I'd first visited, that Harry's behaviour was because of inexperience and had said what she should do. She then said that she had spent thousands on him.

I told her that she should have done what I'd said the first time, in the nicest possible way. She hadn't bothered doing what I had said, but at least she had asked me to come back. Typically, now it was last chance saloon time.

I said that there was only one way I could prove to her whether I was right or wrong and that was to send Harry to Esme. She did.

When she came over to ride Harry, after we'd got him sorted

out, I wouldn't let her ride him at first. I told her to watch Esme on him. Harry was going like a dream for her. I told the lady, "Now you can see how good he really goes, but the minute your bottom (I might have used another word) goes on that saddle, he'll remember it's you. He's not ready for you again, just yet."

Esme continued to ride him and everything went brilliant. The lady came again a couple of days later and this time she got on Harry and you could see his reaction. He initially went, "Oh, flip, it's her again."

But this time she did get it right with Harry, because she listened to Esme. As Esme said, "I had to teach her to ride it."

Harry went back home with the lady who was now doing really well, because she was doing what we had said, but she then brought a woman in to change his bit. Now he's back to Naughty Harry again!

This woman is convinced it's nothing to do with the bit, but that's the only thing that has changed. As Esme says, "Some people just love having problems and it looks like this lady just wants to make life harder than it has to be."

I'm sure some people just want me to say, "You're doing a great job with a quirky horse, you're the hero." Well, maybe I would say that, if they did it right – and some do.

I had this horse I'd seen in West Yorkshire and I'd said that the owner should contact Esme to send it to us at Manor Farm.

I'd said, "We'll give it two or three weeks, which will do it the world of good and I'll treat it as though it was a racehorse." We would get it comfortable, but at the same time out of its comfort zone because it would have had some work, which was its problem. It hadn't had any.

It was only a four-year-old and it just needed some work, that the owner didn't have time to do, and so it was playing up a bit. I said, "If it comes here and sees what work really is like, it will come back to you and think it's on a good thing and behave."

The owner didn't send it. We will probably get it here one day, when it's a last chance saloon again.

We currently have four horses of our own: Captain Mowbray, two of Alex's that we will come to in the next chapter, and one called Royal MacNab (Roy) who came to us from trainer Rebecca Menzies.

Roy had been a successful racehorse, winning three times at Musselburgh and with other wins at Perth and Wetherby. He'd always run well with a lot of top-three finishes, but his career was over.

Rebecca had tried to rehome him. Rebecca has that emotional attachment with her horses and she likes to make sure they all continue to have a good life after their racing is done. Roy had gone to a new owner, but it hadn't worked out and rather than get into any problems or arguments she'd just told the new owner to bring him back. Rebecca then rang me. Could I find him a new home?

I said to bring him down to see what we could do. When Roy arrived I was shocked. Roy was a broken horse, a bit like you'd term a broken man, but I knew it hadn't been Rebecca that had broken him, it had been the people that had rehomed him and they had completely misunderstood him.

That's the advantage I have. I get to understand a horse. I get that sense, that spiritual feeling and along with the knowledge I have, I got him back right and feeling good and we are all having a great time with him now.

He's now Esme's horse and she's done cross country and show jumping with him. I cannot tell you just how much that pleases me. I'd like to think that Rebecca is sharing some of the photos of Roy through her racehorse syndicates about how her wonderful Royal MacNab is enjoying his retirement.

Some people call what I have as intuition. I'm happy with that. It's better than saying the horse has told me.

Rehabilitation is what we do at Manor Farm.

CHAPTER 35

Alex:
Scots Gaelic & Last Encounter

When Alex was a lad, he was a good horseman, he came out of it for a number of years but has now come back and is learning his trade.

He has ambition and has already begun proving himself having worked with a lame horse that also came from Rebecca Menzies, another former successful racehorse Scots Gaelic that won five times, twice over hurdles and three times on the flat.

We've had Scots Gaelic for two years and Alex has brought him back into his ability. The horse is 15 years old now and won't run again, but he has never been lame since Alex got him right and he's now competing in the show ring at RoR.

Alex has what I have. He has that understanding of horses. He listens.

He was also meant to be buying a house, but he must have misunderstood me, or I must have misheard him when I leant him the money because he went out and bought a horse!

I have to say the horse bears no resemblance to a house, that I thought I had given the money towards a deposit, but instead of blowing a gasket with him I just called him a wally!

Last Encounter, the racehorse Alex bought, had quite a successful start to his career in Ireland, winning a Group 1 race at Wexford and with quite a few top-three places and earlier this year was back racing in point-to-point as a 12-year-old. He was second at Sheriff Hutton with jockey Leah Cooper from Husthwaite on board, in April this year (2022).

Alex had bought him from a woman in Herefordshire.

When Last Encounter arrived, I got into my psychic stuff and I found he had been overtrained. All he did when he saw the gallops was become a runaway. He was just gone, whoosh, which was all very good for speed, but he needed stamina too.

The previous owner had said that he was a jack in the box, that he was very nervous. I put that down to him having been galloped every day or at least galloped too much, which meant he'd been overtrained.

People can't believe that a horse doesn't need intensive training, but what it needs is the right training at the right time to suit the horse.

We had him do some road work and then serious hill work. We saw that as better for him than the gallops.

We then took him up to Rebecca Menzies' three weeks before Last Encounter's first race with Alex as trainer. I considered him to be ready to run and you always have to give a horse a run to know where he is, to get a bigger picture.

He jumped off and went a mile and three furlongs in 1 minute 42 seconds. The horse that he was working with was 20–30 lengths behind.

The work rider, who was riding the other horse, got up to the top of the gallop and Last Encounter wasn't even breaking sweat. he said to Alex, who was riding him, that he needed to go again because he wasn't blowing, but that's where people go wrong.

That was a mile and three. If he hadn't been fit, he would certainly have been blowing.

I had said to Alex beforehand not to gallop Last Encounter down the gallops once he'd gone up like that, but to get off him and lead him. If he's not blowing, don't make him blow (for the sake of it). He's fit.

My concern with Last Encounter was that I didn't believe he was a three-miler. He had two-mile form. I reckoned if he got away from some average horses in point-to-point he could dictate his own pace once he'd settled down.

Last Encounter gave it all and more in that point-to-point. But you shouldn't ask a horse to give all and more. This is why I said, "Don't run him again, it's not fair, because he's trying to please, but he can't even though we've got him fit and well."

What we learned by running him at Sheriff Hutton was that he was never going to be quick enough. He'd lost his speed. He'd had it for so long but couldn't maintain it.

We had to stop. It's all about being fair to the horse.

My lad's had some fun with him and he will have fun with others. I'm taking pleasure out of seeing him have that fun as well.

Last Encounter is Alex's first go at training a racehorse. He has a little bit of an ambition about having a horse run at Cheltenham. We all have those dreams. When I was a lad I wanted to ride in the National, but I'm not taking that dream away from him. I'm going to try and help him make it come true.

I've already told Alex that if you have a horse that can get you to Cheltenham you can have pride in simply getting him to the starting line. Anything after that is a bonus, because there are not many that manage it.

And there's another thing about Alex, something that maybe sets him apart from the rest, like me. He reckons he's got somebody around him, a ghost.

This is the grounding with the spiritual world, I got it when I was a child and didn't ignore it. Alex used to have it as a child. He's now got into the horses and is starting to get this gift back. He just needs to listen to the information he is being given.

Alex Cooper – The Second Yorkshire Horseman? Who knows?

CHAPTER 36

Symbols & Colours

I've mentioned voices, messages and intuition. They are involved with my readings, but a lot of it is symbols and colours. It's how I see horses, in symbols and in their energy. Horses, like us, are all hydration, blood circulation and oxygen. Once you've got that everything comes right. I have to read the symbols. And that's where the reiki also helps.

When I'm conducting a reading without seeing the horses I don't get its colour right every time. The colours I sometimes struggle with are a liver chestnut or bright bay, as they are very close.

I once told a woman her horse was grey and she said it wasn't. "Fair enough," I said. "Never mind, we'll keep going," and I continued the reading. Later, when she brought the horse round and I was standing at the gate I asked her what colour it was?

She said, "Flipping heck, it's grey." It was actually a dun but she'd just clipped it and that's what I had been given. I got the symbol of a mushroom for that one.

Universal energy, the guardian angels or spirit guides are hard to explain, but I know that they are there so that I can do right by the horse.

I know how hard it is for some people to believe in the spiritual stuff. As I've said more than once, I would be the biggest cynic if I hadn't been given this gift, and it's something that I know people think can't be possible because they don't live in that frame of mind. It's like, if it's not in this or that bag it's not possible.

I also never believe I'm the best, but there is nobody that I know of who has what I have, my way with horses.

I will say it again. I am not a vet and that I must always advise that if your horse has problems you should always contact your vet.

All I can tell you is that what I get from the universe and the guardian angels, I bring into real life and I help horses. I have to say there are times that I question stuff about messages that I'm given, but I will always say what I see.

What I have learned is not to let others influence you. I know that I can't change every horse. I don't have a pocket full of money and I have learned that I don't need that to be wealthy. I am oozing wealth in how I help.

I know what I have done by listening to messages I have received spiritually, combined with the reiki, combined with my intuition and my horsemanship learned over nearly 60 years, and I know how much my work with horses has done and continues to do. It's those special things. I make a difference. I help horses.

My name is Cooper Wilson – The Yorkshire Horseman.